How War Might Spread to Europe

Miroslav Nincic

sipri

Stockholm International Peace Research Institute

Taylor & Francis
London and Philadelphia
1985

UK	Taylor & Francis Ltd, 4 John St, London WC1N 2ET
USA	Taylor & Francis Inc., 242 Cherry St, Philadelphia, PA 19106–1906

British Library Cataloguing in Publication Data

Nincic, Miroslav
  How war might spread to Europe
  1. War
  I. Title
  355'.02   U21.2

ISBN 0-85066-302-4

Cover design by Malvern Lumsden.
Typeset by Alresford Phototypesetting, Alresford, Hants.
*Printed in Great Britain by Taylor & Francis (Printers) Ltd,
Basingstoke, Hants.*

How War Might Spread to Europe

sipri

Stockholm International Peace Research Institute

SIPRI is an independent institute for research into problems of peace and conflict, especially those of arms control and disarmament. It was established in 1966 to commemorate Sweden's 150 years of unbroken peace.

The institute is financed by the Swedish Parliament. The staff, the Governing Board and the Scientific Council are international.

Governing Board

Rolf Björnerstedt, Chairman (Sweden)
Egon Bahr (FR Germany)
Francesco Calogero (Italy)
Tim Greve (Norway)
Max Jakobson (Finland)
Karlheinz Lohs (German Democratic Republic)
Emma Rothschild (United Kingdom)
The Director

Director

Frank Blackaby (United Kingdom)

sipri

Stockholm International Peace Research Institute
Pipers Väg 28, S-171 73 Solna, Sweden
Cable: Peaceresearch Stockholm
Telephone: 08-55 97 00

Preface

Not many people believe that a war is likely to start in Europe. Europe appears to be a continent with settled boundaries. As the years go by, scenarios of sudden unprovoked incursions across the border either by NATO or Warsaw Treaty Organization troops become less and less plausible.

In many other parts of the world the risks of war are much greater: and in most of these troubled areas the United States and the Soviet Union confront each other by proxy. The possibility cannot be excluded that these indirect conflicts might at some point become direct. Then war might well come to Europe.

In this book Mr Miroslav Nincic of New York University examines these risks. He studies the various areas outside Europe where the major powers—in particular the United States and the Sovet Union—confront each other, and looks at ways in which a war might spread. A final chapter puts forward suggestions about how this risk might be reduced.

This book is part of SIPRI's programme of studies in European Security, a programme under the general direction of Mr Sverre Lodgaard. Acknowledgement is given to William Jewson for editing the manuscript.

SIPRI   *Frank Blackaby*
November 1984   Director

Contents

Acronyms

ALOC	Airlanes of communication
ASW	Anti-submarine warfare
AWACS	Airborne warning and control system
BPA	Basic principles agreement
CENTO	Central Treaty Organization
CMEA	Council for Mutual Economic Assistance
COMEDEAST	Commander eastern Mediterranean (NATO)
CSCE	Conference on Security and Co-operation in Europe
EMP	Electro-magnetic pulse
FAR	Force d'action rapide (France)
GIUK gap	Greenland–Iceland–United Kingdom gap
GLCM	Ground-launched cruise missile
IEPG	Independent European programme group
LRTNF	Long-range theatre nuclear force
NADGE	NATO air defence ground environment
NATO	North Atlantic Treaty Organization
NWFZ	Nuclear weapon-free zone
OPEC	Oil producing and exporting countries
PG/WIO	Persion Gulf/Western Indian Ocean
POL	Petroleum, oil and lubricants (depots)
SALT	Strategic arms limitation talks
SAM	Surface-to-air missile
SLBM	Submarine-launched ballistic missile
SLOC	Sealanes of communication
SSN	Nuclear-propelled submarine
STRIKFORSOUTH	Naval striking and support force southern Europe (NATO)
TLAM-N	Tomahawk land-attack missile—nuclear
TNF	Theatre nuclear forces
USCENTCOM	United States Central Command
WTO	Warsaw Treaty Organization

Chapter 1.   The background: East–West relations and the Third World

I. Introduction

The security and welfare of most European countries on both sides of the Cold War divide are highly sensitive to the quality of US–Soviet relations and to the activities which these two nations engage in beyond their own borders. There are, indeed, few actions or commitments that any European nation might undertake independently that could affect the fate of the continent to the same extent as the external entanglements and the mutual relations of the alliance leaders. Many of these entanglements involve Third World regions and the level of US–Soviet tensions is often determined by competing objectives in these areas.

These statements must, of course, be placed in their historical context before being developed. Each instance of US–Soviet confrontation influences the nature and conduct of subsequent involvements by shaping the circumstances in which they occur. Each confrontation provides a learning experience not only for the protagonists themselves, but also for other nations whose interests are affected by the manner in which the superpowers manage their bilateral relations. It will thus be useful to examine how East–West and North–South relations have interacted in recent decades and to study the issue of European security in this light. In particular, an attempt will be made to show that:

1. Superpower relations are largely, though certainly not exclusively, determined by their fluctuating rivalries in the Third World.
2. The security of many European nations is conditioned by the consequences of these rivalries.

II. Cold Wars, detente and the Third World

It would be wrong to suggest that rivalries in the Third World have been the sole cause of shifts in US–Soviet relations. Other forces, both international and indigenous, have also been at work. Fluctuating national moods and domestic politics, particularly in the USA, have had a significant impact. Events in Europe have also played a role. But to a large extent the history of US–Soviet relations has been conditioned by their competition in the Third World. Relations between the two superpowers have experienced three major surges in hostility since World War II (approximately 1945–52, 1957–63 and 1976 to the present), two plateaux with slight relaxations (1953–57 and 1963–68) and one extended and meaningful period of decreasing tensions (1969–75). This scheme can, in turn, be translated into three major waves of evolving relations: 1945–57, 1957–76 and 1976 to the present. Each shift has been characterized by a specific state of US and Soviet policies in the Third World.

Emergence and consolidation of the Cold War (1945–57)

Various factors have led each of the two wartime allies to regard the other as its most implacable foe. Though events in the Third World contributed to this deterioration in the early post-war years, incompatible objectives within Europe were more important. Differing interpretations of the Yalta agreements—particularly regarding the political future of Poland—appear to have provided the initial impulse for rising hostility. Moreover, the issues of 'free elections' and the form of government that East European nations were to have extended beyond Poland. They came to a head in Czechoslovakia where the forced resignation of President Benes, Jan Masaryk's mysterious death and the consolidation of a Communist government in 1948 produced powerful shockwaves in the West.

Yet even these tensions were intensified by problems originating outside Europe. Iran provided the first major flash-point in the Third World. Iran was occupied by both the USSR and Great Britain during World War II. Towards the end of the war, the USSR refused to withdraw its troops until it, like Britain, had acquired local oil concessions. Under Western pressure Iran refused to grant oil concessions to the USSR and, in response, the USSR backed the creation of an independent republic of Azerbaijan with a pro-Soviet government buttressed by large concentrations of troops on the border. The threat of intervention by the UK and the USA caused Moscow to back down in 1946 but the resulting bitterness and mutual suspicion was to poison subsequent relations. Further strains in the same region grew from Stalin's insistence—based on what he seems to have thought was a promise made by Churchill—on acquiring a Soviet base in the Dardanelles Straits. The USA reacted strongly and President Truman went so far as to dispatch an aircraft-carrier taskforce to Istanbul. The Soviet Union once more backed down while the Cold War was further fuelled. It was given a further boost by the civil strife in Greece as well as by the victory of Mao Tse Tung's forces in China.

In this climate, the position of US statesmen who, like Stimson, Marshal,

Hopkins and Byrnes, had argued against overstating the Soviet threat, was irretrievably weakened. By the same token, the hand of those most eager to place a predatory interpretation on all Soviet activities—Dean Acheson, for example—was considerably strengthened. Hostility towards the Soviet Union thus came to be a firm feature of the US leadership and political structure. The first wave of belligerence crested at the turn of the decade, following the Berlin blockade and the onset of the Korean War. (The Korean War first made a military clash between the two giants a real possibility.) Acheson's failure to include South Korea in the 'defense perimeter' that he described in January 1950 may have emboldened North Korea to launch, six months later, a full-scale invasion. While subsequent evidence has shown that Moscow was probably not behind the decision to invade,[1]* the mood in the USA at the time was beyond an objective assessment of the Soviet role.

Hostility between the superpowers peaked at this stage but levelled off on a temporary plateau or even declined slightly despite the blustering rhetoric of the time. Ideological diatribes continued but acquired a somewhat stale flavour and actual behaviour became more circumspect. Partly due to Eisenhower's fiscal conservatism, the mid-1950s witnessed no major leaps in the arms race. This period saw no significant US–Soviet confrontation in the Third World. This may partly have been a consequence of, but certainly also contributed to, the hiatus in Cold War tensions.

It seems, in fact, that Stalin never had a very strong interest in the Third World.[2] Areas contiguous to the USSR were always much more important to the security-conscious Kremlin. Though the disintegration of colonial empires provided natural opportunities for expanding the Soviet sphere of influence, these opportunities were rarely taken. The military and economic significance of new nations may simply not have sufficed to interest Stalin seriously, and his view that nationalist leaders like Nehru, Gandhi and Sukarno were mere 'imperialist lackeys' may also account for Moscow's apparent inactivity.

Stalin's death in 1953 ushered in a change of attitude, a change that was consolidated by the Third World's emergence as an independent political force after the Bandung Conference of 1955. Khrushchev embraced the non-aligned countries as part of a potential 'zone of peace' and recognized the significance of non-Marxist liberation movements. An increasing amount of Soviet military assistance and even economic aid were directed towards the Middle East (initially Egypt), Asia and, subsequently, Africa as well. The scope for clashing Soviet and US interests was thus expanded.

The second wave and the Third World (1957–76)

A new swell in hostility began to form around 1957. Several circumstances combined to revive a confrontational stance and the Third World played an important part in the process. The launching of Sputnik was a precipitating

* Superscript numbers refer to the list of notes and references at the end of the book.

event. It created a feeling of vulnerability in the USA and a situation in which paranoia could readily thrive. This paranoia had already been aggravated by the Soviet invasion of Hungary. But once again, it was the Third World that furnished both the occasions and the arena for collisions and for the interventionism that this climate gave rise to.

As early as June 1958, 14 000 US troops landed in Lebanon to quell an allegedly Communist-led rebellion and to provide a display of force and will designed to impress Nasser and the United Arab Republic, whose regional influence was so distressing to Washington. The resurging tension was further increased by the approaching US election. Ambitious democrats—including Kennedy, Humphrey and Johnson—used Cold War themes to great advantage throughout their campaigns. They clearly considered that militant statements such as charges of 'missile gaps' and demands for 'expanded deterrence' would help their electoral chances.

Kennedy emerged as the victor and the Third World came to occupy an increasingly central position in US perceptions. Concern with revolutionary movements pervaded the foreign policy agenda and new emphasis was placed on force-projection capabilities. This emphasis included the creation of 'special forces' designed specifically for Third World contingencies.

The first and most important perceived threat originated in Latin America. Castro's successful revolution, with its rapidly apparent Marxist character, was a major jolt to the Kennedy Administration. The United States, whose influence in that small country had previously prevailed, was rebuffed by the new Cuban leadership which moved decisively into the Soviet orbit. A near-obsession with the possibility of radical political transformations in Latin America emerged. This spectre was dealt with by various means, ranging from economic assistance (the Alliance for Progress) to overt military intervention (the Bay of Pigs; the Dominican Republic).

While the upheavals in the Belgian Congo brought the East–West confrontation to sub-Saharan Africa, the most profound consequences at the time were caused by US intervention in Viet Nam. Ever since France's expulsion from the region, US leaders had made constant reference to the 'domino theory'. Viet Nam, Kennedy said, was "the cornerstone of the Free World in Southeast Asia, the keystone of the arch, the finger in the dike . . .".[3] As the number of US troops climbed to half a million, North Viet Nam and the Viet Cong were materially supported by the USSR and, to a much smaller extent, by China. The bitterness associated with Viet Nam created an obstacle to a relaxation of superpower tensions throughout most of the 1960s.

Paradoxically, the most dramatic confrontation in the Third World also provided a major impetus for controlling the most perilous aspects of US–Soviet rivalry. The near-brush with nuclear disaster provoked by the Cuban missile crisis in 1962 initiated a halting movement towards arms control. It also laid certain foundations—such as the Hot Line Agreement—for managing future crises. Indeed, a modest retreat from the second peak of post-war hostility was initiated. Little progress was, however, made for several years. The issue of Viet Nam and, possibly, the Johnson Administration's need to fend off challenges to its domestic programmes from the political right by demonstrating its resolute toughness abroad, hampered real progress until the end of the decade.

Richard Nixon's election created unprecedented opportunities for improved relations. The US public's weariness with foreign military adventures reduced the domestic political risks of a political withdrawal from Viet Nam and the President's anti-Communist credentials protected him from charges of appeasement as he sought to chart a new course in superpower relations. These shifts were further facilitated by the Kremlin's unwillingness to let events in south-east Asia jeopardize Nixon's endeavours.

The two nations embarked on a promising, though ephemeral, period of detente. In addition to the achievements in arms control which the period registered (SALT I and the Vladivostok Accord) and the expansion of commercial and other exchanges between the two sides, a serious attempt was made to develop a basis for non-confrontational relations in the Third World.

As part of what was conceived to be a general road-map for better relations, Nixon and Brezhnev signed a document in May 1972 which was known as the Basic Principles Agreement (BPA).[4] Not only did the agreement state that ideological and social differences should be the object of peaceful negotiations, but it also observed that "Both sides recognise that efforts to obtain unilateral advantages at the expense of the other, directly or indirectly, are inconsistent with these objectives". This provision was taken to refer principally to each side's policy in the developing world. It lacked specificity and its implications have been interpreted differently by the two countries, but it did represent a first attempt to lay the general ground rules for competition in third areas.

A new Cold War (1976 to the present)

It is difficult to identify a definite point at which the detente of the early 1970s yielded to the belligerence of recent years, but the initial impetus probably dates from late in 1973 at the time of the Six Day War. The United States suspected that the Kremlin had prior knowledge of the surprise attack by Egypt and Syria and had, by not alerting Washington, violated the spirit of detente as well as the BPA. This marked a first turning point in superpower relations. Real damage may not have been immediately visible—contacts between the two countries were expanded in 1974 and the Vladivostok Accord was signed in November of that year—but the foundation for continued co-operation had been shaken. This foundation was further undermined by internal political developments in the USA.

The anti-detente and neo-conservative movement that has subsequently shaped much of US foreign policy gained a firm foothold in the national political structure at this time. It included hard-line factions of the Democratic Party as well as the more traditional right-wing forces and advocated Cold War views that the Republican Administration had either muted or abandoned. Grouped in such bodies as the Coalition for a Democratic Majority and the bipartisan Committee on the Present Danger, the movement soon became the most powerful influence on US policy towards the Soviet Union and managed, during much of the remainder of the decade, to block further movement towards co-operation. While such domestic forces were important, it is improbable that they could successfully have scuttled detente had Soviet activities not abetted their efforts. Many of these activities, moreover, directly involved the Third World.

In what may have been a response to the various amendments that finally undermined the US–Soviet trade bill, Cuban troops were encouraged in 1975 to intervene in the Angolan Civil War in support of the Marxist Movimiento Popular de Libertação de Angola (MPLA). The United States in turn expanded its own assistance to União Nacional para a Independência Total de Angola (UNITA) and the Frente Nacional de Libertação de Angola (FNLA), both anti-Soviet forces and rivals of the MPLA. In the 1976 primary elections, and under attack from the Reagan campaign, President Ford formally dropped the word 'detente' from his political vocabulary. Relations were launched on an accelerating downward course and were further undermined by conflicting US–Soviet interests in the Horn of Africa.

The increasingly strong Soviet link to Ethiopia, following the ousting of Haile Selassie by the nominally Marxist government of Mengistu Haile Mariam, also implied the dislodgement of the USA from Ethiopia. In April 1977 Ethiopia's military relationship with Washington was terminated and, in September, Addis Ababa signed a military agreement with the USSR. At the same time, open warfare broke out between Ethiopia and Somalia over the Ogaden region. By late 1977, 14 000 Cuban troops and several hundred Soviet military advisers arrived to assist their client's military efforts.

This provided additional ammunition to those US political elites which had lobbied against detente. Senators Jackson and Baker, for example, suggested that Soviet behaviour in Africa should be considered sufficient grounds for rejecting a new SALT agreement. Pressures even appeared within the Carter Administration for linking arms control to Moscow's behaviour in the Third World. The US reaction notwithstanding, the Soviet and Cuban military presence in Ethiopia was expanded in 1979.

The invasion of Afghanistan on 24 December 1979 definitively terminated a chapter in superpower relations. The tribal rebellion had been gaining momentum and despite the repressive efforts of Hafizullah Amin, who had replaced Mohammad Taraki as Prime Minister, organized unrest was growing in the country. The unrest threatened to undermine the Marxist government and to replace it with a fundamentalist and anti-Soviet Islamic regime. The reasons for the Soviet invasion are open to interpretation but their general outlines are fairly clear. The prospect of an unbroken string of hostile nations—Iran, Afghanistan and China—on the southern flank of the USSR, the fear that Islamic extremism might spread to the country's own

Asian regions and the feeling that SALT II had, in any case, been successfully blocked by US hawks, probably furnished the rationale for a full-scale invasion.

The US response, like that of the rest of the world, was swift, vigorous and bitter. Arms control was in a shambles, the hard-liners felt vindicated and President Carter threatened to meet any further Soviet incursion into the Persian Gulf with military force. Detente's death-knell had sounded. Its actual demise was the culmination of a process whereby the interplay of domestic US politics and superpower regional involvements tore down the edifice constructed in the late 1960s and early 1970s.

It is evident that US–Soviet relations cannot be insulated from the entanglements of the two sides in the Third World. It ought also to be clear that the security of European countries is inextricably bound to this whole complex of relations.

III. The implications for European security

The effects of US–Soviet confrontations in the Third World on European security can manifest themselves in two ways. They can affect the general tenor of East–West relations, and they can provoke specific actions against European nations. The first kind of effect may have been more in evidence in the past but specific actions against European countries may become more frequent and more serious in the future.

Indivisible tension

Inter-alliance tension in Europe has clearly been influenced by Washington's and Moscow's extra-European rivalry. The link has been less of a causal nature than of an interactive, mutually reinforcing one. The consequences for Europe have, nevertheless, been quite substantial. At an early stage of the Cold War, the Kremlin's assumed involvement in the invasion of South Korea was viewed by the USA as evidence of more global designs: "Soviet willingness to use force in Asia was seen, at the least, as applying political pressure in Europe, thereby threatening to undo the US effort to stabilize the Western part of the continent".[5] Because of Korea, US congressional opposition to a conventional military build-up in Europe vanished. The integration of NATO, an increased presence of US troops and expanded military aid to its allies followed. A significant facet of the developing Cold War was the US-sponsored rearmament of the Federal Republic of Germany and the tremors which this caused in the USSR.

The second major surge in East–West enmity of the late 1950s and early 1960s had roots in the Middle East, Africa and Latin America. While Third World issues were obviously not the cause of the major problem in Europe itself—the matter of a divided Germany and of Berlin—they did have an

indirect effect. They served to intensify mutual suspicion and threat perceptions and thus hindered constructive dialogue on the problem of immediate
European concern. The recurring crises over Berlin between 1958 and 1960
brought the opposing blocs closer to actual warfare in Europe than at any
time before or since.

Finally, the third and most recent surge in tension, attributable to a combination of Soviet activity in Africa and political developments in the United
States, has produced significant ramifications for Europe. The major
manifestation of this is the thorny issue of theatre nuclear forces (TNF).
While the problem of TNFs would probably have emerged in the absence of
quarrels in Africa, its negotiated solution would almost certainly have been
easier if the political climate had not been thus poisoned. Again, the security
interests of both NATO and WTO countries have, at least in part, been conditioned by the extra-European disputes of the alliance leaders.

These processes have also operated in reverse. The detente of the late
1960s and early 1970s was facilitated by the superpowers' willingness to mute
their differences in the southern hemisphere which, in turn, encouraged
East–West co-operation in Europe. The Quadripartite Agreement on Berlin
of 1971 was a major beneficiary of, as well as a further contribution to,
improved relations. Negotiations leading to the Conference on Security and
Co-operation in Europe (CSCE) also got under way at this time and economic
exchanges between members of the European Community and Eastern
Europe improved substantially. Thus it can be seen that East–West tension
in Europe is inseparable from East–West tension in the Third World, if
only because they both create and partake of the same overall political
climate.

Specific consequences: the record so far

In addition to the overall relationship between East–West tension in the Third
World and in Europe, individual clashes in non-European regions could have
immediate implications for various European nations. For example, a superpower suffering heavy losses in a Third World conflict at the hands of its rival,
or one to whom such losses seemed imminent, might, if the stakes were high
enough, compensate by taking military action against the other superpower's
interests elsewhere. There are circumstances in which this could involve parts
of Europe.

Such a threat was present during the Cuban missile crisis in October 1962.
Since the US naval position in the Caribbean was vastly superior to that of the
USSR, and since air strikes against Cuba could easily be launched from the
US mainland, military action to remove the Soviet missiles could, in principle,
have been successfully undertaken. Consequently it was feared that the
USSR might retaliate against NATO countries in regions where its own
logistical position was more favourable. Berlin, isolated 175 kilometres inside

the German Democratic Republic, was an obvious possibility. In anticipation of the danger, 'precautionary measures' were taken by the West German government in order to bolster the 'defence readiness' of the country's armed forces. The allied military presence was strengthened while Berlin households began stocking food.[6] In addition, a message from Khrushchev to Kennedy on 28 October carried the implied threat of an invasion of Turkey, a NATO member, if Cuba were attacked.[7] In the end a military confrontation was averted, but the crisis dramatically illustrated the possible consequences of such situations for Europe. Dangers of this sort increase with the geographical indivisibility of either side's military strategy and recent trends in military doctrine are disquieting in this regard.

US–Soviet confrontations in the Third World need not necessarily invite actions against European nations only on the part of the rival superpower. Local parties to the conflict might, for example, seek to retaliate against countries which are, even if only indirectly, associated with the hostilities. A case in point is the Six Day War of 1973. On that occasion the USA supplied weapons to Israel using NATO bases in Western Europe as transport points. In response, the Arab members of OPEC (Oil Producing and Exporting Countries) imposed an embargo that threatened severe damage to a number of West European economies.

Most relevantly, perhaps, a European ally of either alliance leader may find itself involved, directly or indirectly, in its leader's regional conflicts and thus have to bear all the associated perils and costs. The bulk of this study will examine the circumstances in which such involvements could occur in the future. It is worth noting that the actual historical record is largely blank. Neither the European members of NATO nor their WTO counterparts have been drawn into their leader's Third World adventures either at all frequently or at all meaningfully. Token contributions were furnished by a few allies to the US interventionary force in Korea, but so far things have not gone much further than this.

When the USA considered intervening in order to shore up the French position at Dien Bien Phu—probably by air strikes, possibly even with nuclear weapons—efforts were made to enlist British support as well. Nothing came of this however. Churchill was not interested and the US Senate was unenthusiastic. In fact, in the immediate post-war decades, it was more usual for European powers to seek US support for their external policies than vice versa. Frequently they were unsuccessful. In the case of the Dutch East Indies (the Republic of Indonesia since independence in 1949) the USA did not support the Netherlands, nor did it support Dutch claims to West Irian (which Indonesia acquired in 1962). The Anglo-French attack on Egypt, which followed Nasser's decision to nationalize British and French investment in the Suez Canal, provoked major acrimony within the Atlantic Alliance as the USA acted against the invasion in the United Nations. The USA actually cut off oil supplies from Latin America that were needed by the

UK and France to replace the lost Middle Eastern oil.[8] Subsequent relations
between France and the USA were not helped by Washington's unwillingness
to endorse the war against Algerian independence.

Taken as a whole, the record indicates that for a significant period the USA
did more to avoid being drawn into the Third World entanglements of its
allies than it did to involve the allies in its own entanglements. Clearly things
have changed considerably since the early post-war decades. European
interests in the Third World have shrunk relative to those of the USA while
the US military reach has expanded considerably. As a consequence, the past
may prove a very imperfect guide to the future—particularly if current trends
in US strategic and foreign policy are taken into account. In order to place
the situation in its new context, two developments must be fully considered:
(*a*) the deterioration of US–Soviet relations in recent years; and (*b*) the new
military doctrines and deployments that have accompanied this deterioration.

The new political setting

Both the *scope* of US–Soviet rivalry and its *intensity* have increased since the
demise of detente in the late 1970s.

The growing scope of rivalry has meant that it has spread to regions that
were previously considered peripheral to the external interests of the
superpowers. Apart from Cuba, the USSR had previously restricted its forays
into the Third World to contiguous Asian areas and to the Middle East. But
during the past decade it has shown a greater readiness to seek advantages,
albeit at low military risk, in more distant parts of the developing world. For
the USA, virtually all parts of the globe now seem relevant to the nation's
geostrategic objectives. Rivalry has also come to encompass an increasing
number of contentious matters as new economic and political issues have
been added to what was already a substantial inventory.

The heightened intensity of the rivalry is reflected in the unusually pug-
nacious posturing and the flaccid efforts to seek co-operative solutions to
common problems. Rhetoric has not quite attained the frenzied pitch of the
late 1940s and early 1950s, but it stands in sharp contrast to the constructive
moderation of the late 1960s and early 1970s, and the new hostility
encourages each side to place as predatory an explanation as possible on the
activities of the other.

Certain implications of these trends suggest themselves. The widening
scope, both geographical and substantive, of the rivalry increases the range of
European interests that could be caught up in the resulting conflicts. The
heightened animosity could make ensuing crises difficult to manage, and their
spread and costs may thus be more devastating.

The following chapters will deal with specific geographic areas, the stakes
involved in the conflict and scenarios of European involvement. The military
conceptions which have recently been applied to East–West relations should
be outlined at the outset.

The new military context

Different phases in US–Soviet relations have typically been characterized by shifting force postures and strategic doctrines. Such shifts have been particularly evident on the US side. Perhaps the most novel and significant strands of current military thinking concern the increasing range of contingencies to which armed force is considered appropriate and the expanding role that is attributed to nuclear weaponry. These two strands are, moreover, mutually entangled.

The functions currently assigned to nuclear arms are more extensive and varied than ever before. They go far beyond the 'massive retaliation' advocated in the Eisenhower years, Kennedy's 'flexible response' and McNamara's 'mutual assured destruction' or the countervailing and counterforce doctrine of the Ford and Carter incumbencies. Indeed, a major complaint of the Reagan Administration against former policies is that "Although U.S. military strategy has deterred direct Soviet attack for many years, it has not prevented indirect incursions within the less developed world".[9] And since "Conflict involving the Soviet Union could occur anywhere on the globe, U.S. military strategy must concern itself with contingencies in all regions of the world".[10]

As a consequence, armed force, including nuclear weaponry, must be able to perform a much greater variety of missions than had previously been thought appropriate since deterrence must obtain "at all points along the spectrum of violence and be integrated from region to region".[11]

Much of this thinking was initially incorporated into the US five-year Defense Guidance Plan in 1982. The plan anticipated the possibility of a 'protracted' nuclear or conventional conflict in which the United States must be sure to "prevail" and "be able to seek earliest termination of hostilities on terms favorable to the United States".[12]

The metaphor behind the strategy is that of a 'continuum' or 'seamless web' between levels of violence and geographical areas. This necessitates a US capacity for 'escalation dominance', that is, an ability to respond in all circumstances with a slightly greater level of violence than the adversary.[13] Above all, gaps in levels of possible response must be avoided, for if the Kremlin thought that a provocation could only be met with a disproportionately more destructive countermove, it might consider such a response unlikely and hence not be deterred. Moreover, this capacity must be global in extent. "United States forces might be required simultaneously in geographically separate theaters"[14] such as Europe, south-west Asia and east Asia. In each case the USA must be able to confront the USSR with the prospect of as destructive a conflict as it may choose to impose.

The desired continuum in levels of violence in turn implies the integration of various forms of weaponry. Integrated plans for using long-, medium- and short-range nuclear arms have been developed and the procurement of new 'dual-capable' (conventional and nuclear) weaponry has been emphasized.[15]

Stress has also been put upon improved conventional and chemical weapons and there has been focus on the highly mobile and flexible sea-launched cruise missiles (SLCM) which can be mounted with nuclear warheads on either submarines or surface ships and which can have land-attack missions (making them well suited for regional conflicts).[16]

The doctrine of the USA on these matters is quite explicit. That of the USSR, because of the closed nature of the society, is highly secret. Beyond a professed disbelief in the possibility of controlling levels of nuclear destruction, little has been published or said within the Soviet Union to illuminate the role, if any, assigned to nuclear weapons in local conflicts. It is nevertheless evident, as will be discussed in chapter 2, that the Soviet military presence in the Third World has expanded in recent years. It can also be inferred that several theatre nuclear systems, and specifically the SS-20 missiles and Backfire bombers deployed in the southern part of the USSR, may be intended to preserve nuclear options in portions of the Third World.

These developments, in tandem with increased East–West tension, carry several implications. To begin with, the attempt to develop a military response for virtually every political or military contingency vastly expands the set of situations under which armed force might be used. It is reasonable to conclude that the probability of an armed conflict has increased—all the more so given the current level of US–Soviet tension. In addition, the built-in continuum from conventional to strategic nuclear warfare reduces the significance of military 'firebreaks' and psychological barriers to an all-out escalation of such conflicts as might occur.

The implications for most European nations are, in turn, not reassuring:

1. As the range of possible conflicts grows, the probability that the external interests of European countries will be involved in the superpowers' Third World confrontations increases as well.

2. The possibility of rapidly escalating conflicts means that the destruction to which Europe might fall victim could be particularly severe.

In sum, the link between European security and US–Soviet rivalries in the Third World can no longer be viewed in terms that might have been appropriate a mere decade ago. The next two chapters will undertake a more detailed examination of this link by considering the major Third World arenas in which the interests of the superpowers may collide and by discussing various scenarios positing direct or indirect European involvement.

Chapter 2. The arenas: superpower disputes and the Third World

I. Introduction

There have been a number of predictable features of the rivalry between the United States and the Soviet Union in the Third World. Whenever significant economic or strategic interests attach to a country or region, when the country or region is not unambiguously within one side's recognized sphere of interest and when the country or region is marked by a measure of conflict or instability, one or both superpowers will typically try to establish a local presence at the other's expense. Rivalry and escalating tension are the inevitable outcome.

Although the security of European countries is conditioned by US–Soviet relations, there is no simple formula linking this security to the vicissitudes of the superpowers' competition in the Third World. The implications for Europe of these disputes will, to a large extent, depend on their geographical setting. On the one hand, the coincidence of interests between a European nation and those of the USA or the USSR will vary from one part of the world to another. Logistic considerations also make European involvements more plausible in certain regions than in others. To set the stage for further discussion, the principal arenas of superpower rivalry in the Third World must be described. The regional stakes should be identified and the military contexts of the disputes explained. The ramifications of these rivalries for European countries can then be examined.

No part of the Third World at present seems to offer greater likelihood of superpower clashes than the region comprising the Persian Gulf and the western Indian Ocean (PG/WIO). The following section will therefore attempt to outline the issues associated with that part of the world. The eastern Mediterranean is also a troubled area but one which is better understood on account of its longer history of conflict and contention. This area will also be examined, though in less detail. Other regions of significant US–Soviet strife that could, directly or indirectly, affect European security will then be discussed.

II. The Persian Gulf and the Indian Ocean

The PG/WIO area has never been irrelevant to the foreign policy calculations of either superpower but it is now more central to their interests than ever before. As lat as 1977 both sides maintained a relatively modest military presence in the area and during the early days of the Carter Administration there was even serious talk of a treaty to demilitarize the Indian Ocean. By 1978 the situation had changed dramatically. The conflict in the Horn of Africa underscored the regional rivalry of the two superpowers. The fall of the Shah in Iran weakened the USA's position in the Persian Gulf and increased local political uncertainty. The Soviet invasion of Afghanistan enhanced the perceived military threat to US regional interests.

Mutual hostility frequently acquires its own dynamics and antagonism often seems to outrun the contested issues. There is, nevertheless, a sense in which the interests of the superpowers in the PG/WIO may be considered objectively incompatible. The oil reserves of the Persian Gulf, the mineral wealth of nations elsewhere in the Indian Ocean and the crucial sealanes of communication (SLOC) within the region provide major stakes of US–Soviet rivalry.

The stakes

The major US economic interest in the area involves oil. The USA is less dependent on external sources of oil than are its principal allies but it remains somewhat vulnerable. Approximately 20 per cent of domestic oil consumption was met from foreign sources in 1983. Ten per cent of imports were from OPEC nations.[17] The figures reflect a period of exceptionally low external dependence largely occasioned by the economic slowdown. As recovery sets in the nations of the Persian Gulf are likely to provide a larger share of US energy needs and an interruption of oil shipments could cause real economic disarray.[18] If oil supplies from this area to most other Western democracies were disrupted, the damage to international trade and the threat to financial markets would be a matter of very serious concern to the United States.

Beyond the Persian Gulf, but within the area of the Indian Ocean, lie countries whose importance to the USA stems from their possession of economically and militarily vital minerals. The Republic of South Africa is particularly important as a supplier of crucial raw materials to the USA. The major minerals involved are chromium, manganese, vanadium and platinum.[19]

Chromium is used as an alloy to augment the hardness of steel and to enhance its resistance to oxidation and corrosion. In this function it has no known substitute and is thus essential in numerous industrial and military applications, for example the production of tool steel and several jet-engine parts. Imports account for over 90 per cent of US needs. The largest deposits of chromium in the Third World are located in the Republic of South Africa and Zimbabwe. These two countries account for the bulk of US imports.

Manganese is also vital to the steel industry and is sometimes alloyed with aluminium, magnesium and copper. The USA is again almost entirely dependent on foreign sources for this metal.

Vanadium is used as an addition to iron and steel and is especially important in applications where weight reduction is a major consideration. Vanadium is also used to produce titanium alloys and these have important military applications. South Africa supplies over half the vanadium imported by the United States.

Platinum-group metals are used as catalysts in automobile emission-control systems which exist on virtually all US cars. They are also used in the chemical industry and in petroleum refining. South Africa is the United States' major supplier of imported platinum.

Zambia and Zaire are major suppliers of both copper and cobalt to the USA. While they are not Indian Ocean nations themselves, much of their minerals are transported to South Africa for shipment abroad. Madagascar and India, both of which are Indian Ocean nations, are major suppliers of mica to the USA. Mica, though admittedly not an essential raw material, is nevertheless a very useful one. Thus, as regards both oil and non-fuel minerals, the PG/WIO region is of major economic importance to the USA.

There are two ways in which the USSR could be perceived as a threat to US raw-material supplies. In the first place, the Soviet Union could also become dependent on external sources for these same materials and might seek access to sources at the expense of the USA. In the second place, Moscow could seek to deny the USA access to these resources, irrespective of its own needs, with the aim of weakening its principal adversary. Either scenario could have serious implications and their plausibility should therefore be examined.

At present the Soviet Union does not rely significantly on imports of these commodities. It currently produces virtually all the oil that it consumes and is, indeed, a net exporter of petroleum. In 1977 the Central Intelligence Agency (CIA) predicted a sharp decline in Soviet oil production. (This was attributed mainly to an anticipated slowdown of production from the West Siberian field.[20]) But the CIA has since revised these predictions and now believes that the Soviet Union's oil future is reasonably good.[21] The USSR is not, in any case, excessively dependent on this particular source of energy and an expanded reliance on natural gas or on nuclear power could reduce the role of petroleum in the country's economy. Even if some of the bleaker predictions of future Soviet oil production were to be borne out, current levels of exports should provide a comfortable cushion for domestic needs. Thus, although the East European allies may have to turn elsewhere for much of their petroleum—or rely more on alternative sources of energy—the USSR itself could remain relatively self-sufficient for some time to come. It therefore seems unlikely that the two superpowers would, in the foreseeable future, be propelled into conflict by competing needs for Persian Gulf oil.

What can be said of possible conflicts over access to *non-fuel minerals* in South Africa or elsewhere in the region? Some observers consider this a salient issue. For example, Alexander Haig announced in 1980 that: "As one assesses the recent stepup of Soviet proxy activity in the Third World . . . then one can only conclude that the era of the 'resource war' has arrived".[22] However, the Soviet Union is far less dependent on external sources for the minerals which it consumes than is the USA (see table 1).[23] Bauxite is one of the few minerals for which the Soviet Union is heavily dependent on imports. The major sources of supply are, in order of importance, Guinea, Yugoslavia, Hungary and India. Only India is part of the region under consideration and is, in any case, only a marginal supplier.

Table 1.   Net import reliance of the USA and the USSR as a percentage of consumption for selected raw materials

	USA	USSR
Titanium (rutile)	100	0
Columbium	100	0
Mica (sheet)	100	0
Manganese	98	0
Bauxite	94	39
Cobalt	91	42
Chromium	90	0
Tantalum	91	0
Platinum-group metals	85	0
Tin	80	24
Asbestos	80	0
Nickel	72	0
Zinc	67	0
Cadmium	63	0
Tungsten	52	14
Selenium	49	0

Source: US Department of Defense, *Report of the Secretary of Defense Caspar W. Weinberger to the Congress, Fiscal Year 1985* (US Government Printing Office, Washington, D.C., 1984), p. 96.

The Soviet Union relies on imports for 42 per cent of its domestic requirements of cobalt although, paradoxically, it exports cobalt to other member countries of the CMEA (Council for Mutual Economic Assistance). The major foreign supplier is Cuba and the USSR also imports cobalt from Zaire and Zambia. Cobalt is thus the only mineral over which the superpowers could plausibly compete. But Soviet external dependence is not great enough and the proportion of supplies from non-Cuban sources not sufficiently significant for resource conflicts over cobalt to be really likely in the foreseeable future.

The situation regarding the critical minerals supplied to the United States by South Africa is even less threatening. The USSR is the second largest producer and exporter of chromite, after South Africa, and its manganese industry is the largest in the world—in fact the Soviet Union is a supplier of

Figure 1. Superpower access to military facilities in the PG/WIO area

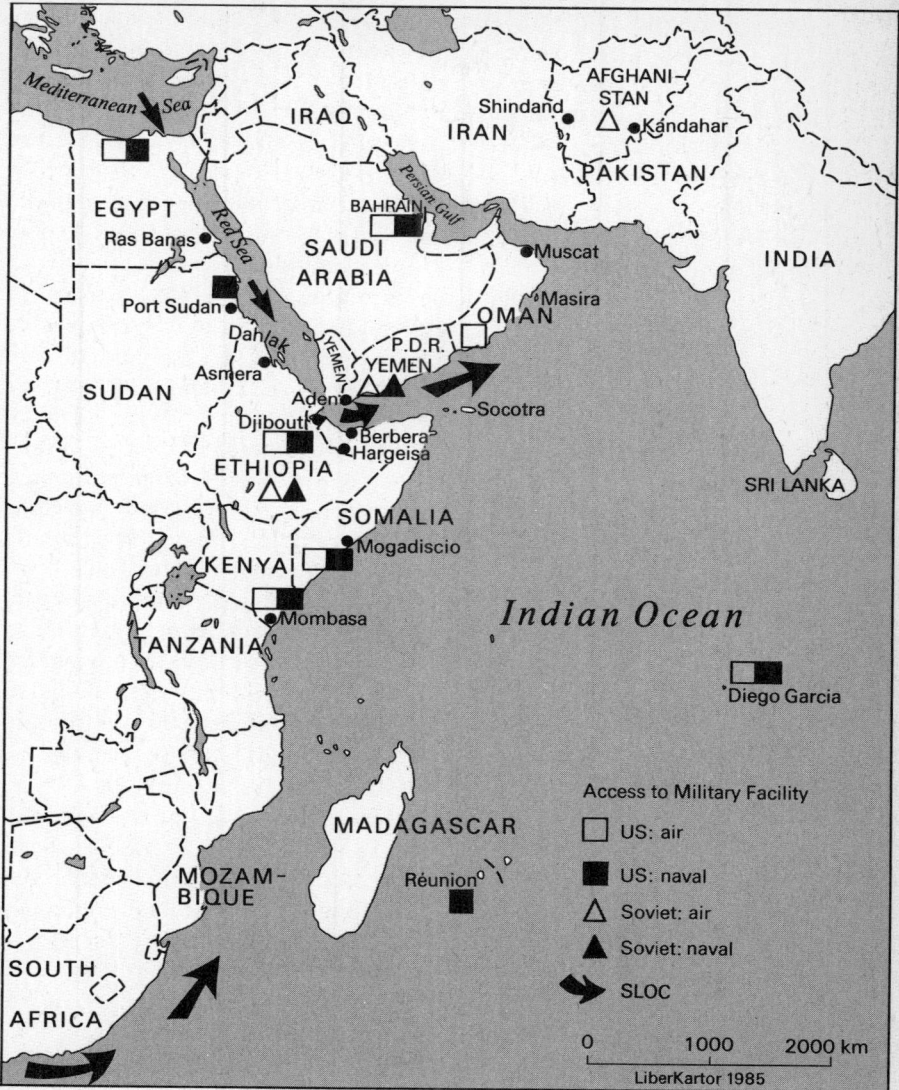

Note: Symbols do not indicate exact locations nor exact numbers of facilities in each country.

both of these metals to the United States. It is also a substantial exporter of platinum-group metals—much of it again to the USA—and, to a lesser extent, of vanadium.

The notion of superpower confrontations over access to oil or non-fuel minerals needed by both nations is, on the whole, implausible. The second scenario dealing with attempted resource *denial*, in a situation of acute tensions or actual conflict, is somewhat more credible. What makes such a scenario conceivable in the PG/WIO area is the fact that, quite apart from its valuable resources, the area lies astride certain vital sealanes of communication (figure 1). Thus, even in the absence of major crises, local beachheads are valuable to each side's geostrategic position.

One major maritime route links Europe to Asia and East Africa via the Mediterranean, the Red Sea and the Indian Ocean. Another route provides for the shipment of oil from the Persian Gulf to the Indian Ocean through the Straits of Hormuz and, from there, to much of the industrialized world. The Cape Route, a very important sea route, links the Indian Ocean to the South Atlantic, and is used to ship goods and commodities to the USA and Western Europe. These SLOCs (sealanes of communication) are of considerable economic and strategic importance and each of them is vulnerable to disruption.[24] For example, naval targets within the north-west Indian Ocean—where these three major SLOCs intersect—are within range of Soviet Backfire bombers based in southern Afghanistan. The Mozambique Channel is only 400 kilometres wide at its narrowest point between Mozambique and Madagascar and therefore qualifies as a major choke-point on the Cape Route. Soviet attempts to gain facilities in Mozambique and US success in doing so in Kenya may partially be interpreted in this light.

While competing domestic needs for minerals would imply attempts to gain control of their sources, a strategy of resource denial can be implemented by controlling either the actual sources of the minerals or the SLOCs by which they are shipped. The significance of fears concerning resource denial is clearly related to the overall state of US–Soviet relations, and their sharp deterioration since the late 1970s largely accounts for the militarization of the Persian Gulf and the Indian Ocean. In addition, the instability of many governments within the region increases the stakes as well as the scope of possible superpower clashes.

The upheaval in Iran has increased US concern for the viability of other allies in the Persian Gulf. Doubts about the longevity of the Saudi regime—particularly since the events surrounding the Grand Mosque in Mecca (which was occupied by Sunni Muslim extremists for two weeks in 1979)—are compounded by uncertainties regarding the stability of Sultan Qabus' rule in Oman. Regional conflicts increase the political volatility of the Gulf area. Although neither superpower appears to be deeply involved in the Iran–Iraq war, a spread of hostilities to neighbouring countries could affect the local interests of both Moscow and Washington. Political instability in the PG/WIO region is, moreover, not limited to the Persian Gulf.

The contradictions and tensions surrounding South Africa's racial policies make future violence and instability virtually inevitable. Namibia's unresolved political future and South Africa's hostile relations with its neighbours further contribute to making this an area marked as much by the explosive nature of its politics as by its resources of vital minerals. Some superpower competition for local footholds is therefore to be expected.

The Soviet occupation of Afghanistan, coupled with US concern over the stability and independence of Pakistan, make south-west Asia another peril-ridden region. The region's contiguity to the Persian Gulf accentuates its importance.

In sum, the richness of its natural resources, the presence of vital SLOCs and the political volatility of the surrounding countries combine to make the PG/WIO a region in which US–Soviet confrontation is a constant possibility. Both superpowers have embarked on a scramble for allies, bases and staging posts and have undertaken major naval deployments in the region.

US–Soviet military presence

Deployments in the PG/WIO area are linked to the task of ensuring access to oil and non-fuel minerals as well as to the SLOCs by which they are trans-ported to the USA and its allies. The expansion of military activities has, moreover, moved in tandem with the steady deterioration in US–Soviet rela-tions since the late 1970s. The USA's determination to increase its armed pre-sence in the area stemmed initially from the 1978 conflict in the Horn of Africa and from the turmoil in Iran that resulted in the loss of its major Persian Gulf ally. Both these events occurred at a time of growing US dependence on foreign oil. US threat perceptions were further exacerbated by the Soviet invasion of Afghanistan and a national consensus soon formed on the need for a military capacity to deal with threats in this part of the world.

A first initiative, and one around which other military projects revolved, was the creation of the Rapid Deployment Force.[25] Its stated purpose was to provide the capacity for the rapid projection of armed force in the PG/WIO region for reasons of deterrence, combat and diplomatic pressure. The Rapid Deployment Joint Task Force was chartered on 1 October 1981 and upgraded to become the United States Central Command (USCENTCOM) on 1 January 1983 with headquarters at Macdill Air Force Base in Florida.

The force, which is drawn from all four services, involves well over 200 000 troops. It includes one airborne division, one airmobile/air assault division, one mechanized infantry division, one light infantry division, one air cavalry brigade, an augmented marine amphibious force, seven tactical fighter wings, two strategic bomber squadrons, three carrier battle groups, one surface action group and five maritime patrol air squadrons. Some of the forces are permanently stationed in the USA while others are deployed elsewhere, notably in Europe, the Pacific and the Indian Ocean itself. To ensure quick reaction time and long-range force-projection capacity, the programme includes procurement of a new long-range, medium-sized cargo aircraft designed to operate from short and rather primitive airfields. The programme also provides for new roll-on/roll-off cargo ships to hold equipment for the marine amphibious force. In the meantime, equipment is pre-stocked aboard cargo ships moored at Diego Garcia. This coral island in the middle of the Indian Ocean has been leased from Great Britain by the USA and possesses a port and an airfield. The installations are being upgraded for forward deployment purposes; however, Diego Garcia lies some 3 400 km from the Straits of Hormuz and it has thus been considered necessary to acquire facilities less distant from the Persian Gulf.

The United States has also obtained access to the Kenyan port of Mombasa and to the Somalian port of Berbera. (Berbera was initially developed by the Soviet Union before it was ousted from Somalia and, besides the port, contains an airfield as well.) The USA makes use of port facilities in Djibouti and enjoys access to the Somalian airfield at Hargeisa. In Oman, an airfield has been developed for US needs on the island of Masira, which used to be a British base, and a facility at Muscat has been upgraded. The USA also has access to bases at Thumrait and Khasab. A naval presence is maintained in Bahrain and the United States has access to naval facilities in Port Sudan, Mogadiscio and on the French island of Réunion.[26]

Although the Rapid Deployment Force—now USCENTCOM—was to draw naval forces from fleets in other seas—the Second Fleet in the Atlantic, the Sixth Fleet in the Mediterranean, the Third Fleet in the eastern Pacific and the Seventh Fleet in the western Pacific—naval deployments have been increased in the PG/WIO itself. In the 1970s, when the Persian Gulf squadron represented the only US military presence in the region, it amounted to three destroyers. The USA now stations some 23 ships in the area, including 2 carriers and 16 surface combatants as well as over 100 fighter attack planes. Four warships are permanently based at Bahrain.

The USA has also conducted major military exercises in the area as a demonstration of military capability and resolve. The biggest of these so far was operation Bright Star, which was centred on the Egyptian desert but also included Oman, Somalia and the Sudan. More than 7 000 US military personnel from the four services participated.[27]

The Soviet Union has not been idle in the area either. Geographic proximity to both the Persian Gulf and south-west Asia implies that a major force-projection capability along the lines adopted by the USA would not be required by the USSR.[28] The nearest Soviet analogue is an airborne force of seven divisions and about 7 000 men. Of these divisions, only two are stationed in the Soviet Union's southern military district and appear to be available for immediate external deployment. The others would have to be flown south before being deployed. The Soviet airlift fleet is composed of 100 Il-76s (comparable to the US C-141), 50 An-22s (the only Soviet aircraft capable of carrying tanks) and 550 An-12 aircraft. The An-12 is an old model—it first entered into service in 1959—with a range of only 1 350 kilometres. (The civilian airline Aeroflot could presumably also make a contribution to an airlift.) The Soviet airlift capacity does not really appear equal to the task of conducting major force-projection operations and could currently be effective only on a rather limited basis. Soviet amphibious capacity in the region is also modest at present although the first Ivan Rogov-class amphibious ship—three times the size of previous amphibious ships—was observed deployed in the Indian Ocean in 1981.

As a US military analyst recently pointed out: "At present the Soviet Union possesses only minimal capabilities to project and sustain military power far from her borders". And further: "As we assess the prospects for future improvements in Soviet force projection capabilities, we find rather modest effort in areas that would support direct force projection into distant places".[29]

Although the Soviet capacity to launch distant and extensive operations in the face of military resistance is limited by airlift and sealift constraints, Moscow does have the ability to threaten SLOCs that are economically vital to the United States and its allies. The invasion of Afghanistan has improved the USSR's strategic position in the region. Several airfields in southern Afghanistan have been put into military service, placing the Persian Gulf within range of Soviet tactical aircraft and, incidentally, reducing the distance to Ethiopia and South Yemen as well.[30] Moreover, Backfire bombers operating from these positions could, as previously observed, imperil naval targets in the north-west part of the Indian Ocean. In addition, the pattern of foreign military footholds which the Soviet Union has sought appear to be linked to the mission of controlling the SLOCs by which major commodities are shipped.

Following the outbreak of the Iran–Iraq war, the Soviet Indian Ocean squadron grew to roughly 30 vessels, including about a dozen combat ships. (Inadequate base facilities have forced the USSR to maintain a rather high ratio of support ships to warships in the PG/WIO.) The USSR has also sought naval facilities, and airfields where possible, within the region. These efforts initially focused on South Yemen, which lies along the Bab-al-Mandab Strait, a strategic choke-point between the Red Sea and the Indian Ocean. The Soviet Union has obtained an installation at Socotra, a South Yemen island in the Arabian Sea, and also enjoys port facilities and access to an airfield in Aden.[31]

In addition, the Soviet Union has undertaken construction of naval facilities, including submarine pens, in the Dahlak Islands off the Ethiopian port of Massa. (Ethiopia is, of course, located on the other side of the Bab-al-Mandab Strait.) The Soviet Union has also acquired access to air facilities at Asmara. However, not all ventures of this sort have been successful. Moscow has, for example, reportedly sought to acquire bases in the Maldives and in Madagascar but has, in both cases, been rebuffed.[32]

The forces deployed by both superpowers in this area have a strong nuclear component. The United States' aircraft carriers in the Indian Ocean carry nuclear weapons, as do over 80 per cent of the large surface ships.[33] Sea-launched land-attack cruise missiles are becoming a major component of nuclear force in USCENTCOM's area of responsibility. And of course, many targets in the PG/WIO are within range of nuclear-equipped Soviet Backfire bombers and SS-20 missiles.

Conclusion

Thus, an area that had previously had very little significance for superpower rivalry is now a major cauldron within which disputes and possible clashes are constantly brewing. It is not, however, the only flashpoint of conflict which could seriously affect European security. Other such arenas exist too, most notably the eastern Mediterranean, a region whose fate is, in some ways, linked to that of the PG/WIO.

III. *The eastern Mediterranean*

While the PG/WIO area is a most likely locus of future superpower clashes in the Third World, in the recent past the eastern Mediterranean has been the most volatile area. The eastern Mediterranean will probably continue as another source of threats to world peace in the years to come, both because of the region's own problems and because of its links to those of the Persian Gulf.

It was in this area of the Third World that US–Soviet competition first became heated. The USSR undertook arms shipments to Egypt from 1955 and the USA's refusal to assist with the Aswan Dam project in 1956 brought the Egyptians even closer to the Soviet Union. The diplomatic defeat of Britain and France in the Suez crisis, and subsequent US fears of a vacuum into which the Kremlin might step, reinforced Washington's decision to involve itself in the region. This decision was enshrined in the Eisenhower Doctrine which, in 1958, was invoked to justify US military intervention in Lebanon.

Soviet arms transfers came to include Syria and, eventually, Libya, Iraq, the People's Republic of Yemen and even the PLO. The USA supplied arms to Israel, Jordan and, after Sadat's break with Moscow, Egypt.[34]

The Middle East wars of 1967 and 1973 raised at least the possibility of a US–Soviet armed confrontation. Soviet naval deployments increased substantially with the June war and the US Sixth Fleet adopted a very visible posture. It was at that time that the Hot Line between Washington and Moscow—installed by agreement in 1963—was used for the first time. During the Six Day War, Moscow airlifted military supplies to its Arab friends and again increased its naval presence in the region. Soviet submarines and warships were, in fact, concentrated close to US aircraft carriers and amphibious units. On 24 October, apparently fearing a unilateral Soviet move to enforce the three-day-old cease-fire, the USA called a world-wide alert of its armed forces. Seven Soviet airborne divisions had by then also been placed on alert.

Ultimately, both sides tried to steer away from the brink of confrontation by restraining their respective clients. Nonetheless, they came uncomfortably close to the precipice. As the US Chief of Naval Operations later observed: "I doubt that major units of the U.S. Navy were ever in a tenser situation since World War II ended . . .".[35]

The interests of both superpowers in the eastern Mediterranean run deep and their nature is not exclusively economic or military. Most notably, US commitments to Israel stem partly from the latter's position as the only Western-style democracy in the area and from the demands of internal US politics. There are, nevertheless, several pragmatic, geostrategic reasons for Washington's and Moscow's efforts to establish their local influence.

Developments in Arab–Israeli relations have unavoidable implications for the Persian Gulf and hence for the security of oil supplies. Moreover, a portion of the oil destined for Western Europe is shipped via the Mediterranean and the Suez Canal, which is a vital point of access for Europe to the Indian Ocean. The USSR also conducts a significant amount of its maritime traffic in the Mediterranean.

In addition, the region also includes Turkey and Greece, the two NATO members which constitute the southern flank of the Atlantic alliance. These two countries represent something to be protected for one of the superpowers and something to be guarded against for the other. The presence of US nuclear-armed submarines endows the region with a strategic, as well as a conventional military significance. The increased deployment of naval cruise missiles further accentuates the militarization of the region, as does the deployment of ground-launched cruise missiles in Sicily. The Soviet Mediterranean squadron carries, or has available, nuclear anti-ship cruise missiles and anti-submarine warfare weapons. The USA (in addition to 2–3 SSBNs) has some 300 nuclear warheads deployed in the Mediterranean in land-attack, anti-air and anti-submarine weapons.

The political volatility of the eastern Mediterranean is unlikely to decrease in the near future: the causes of instability are too numerous and too deeply rooted. Despite occasional surges of optimism, the Arab–Israeli conflict does not seem to be heading towards a definitive settlement. Some momentum was generated by the Camp David Agreement and this did lead to Israel's withdrawal from Sinai. But there has been virtually no progress on the issue of the Golan Heights nor, more fundamentally, on the Palestinian problem. Even if Jordan's full adherence were to be acquired, Israel's resistance to the concept of an authentic Palestinian homeland remains. Were Israel to yield on the issue, the aspiration of many Palestinians for fully fledged statehood could make the notion of a homeland, without all of the attributes of national sovereignty, an unstable solution in the long run.

There are other ways in which a resolution of the Arab–Israeli conflict might prove ephemeral. For example, a successful bid for power by fundamentalist Muslims in Egypt—or even a significant increase in their political authority within the nation—could make it harder for Cairo to be a continuing party to the peace process in the Middle East. Explosive conflicts between

Figure 2. Superpower access to military facilities in the eastern Mediterranean

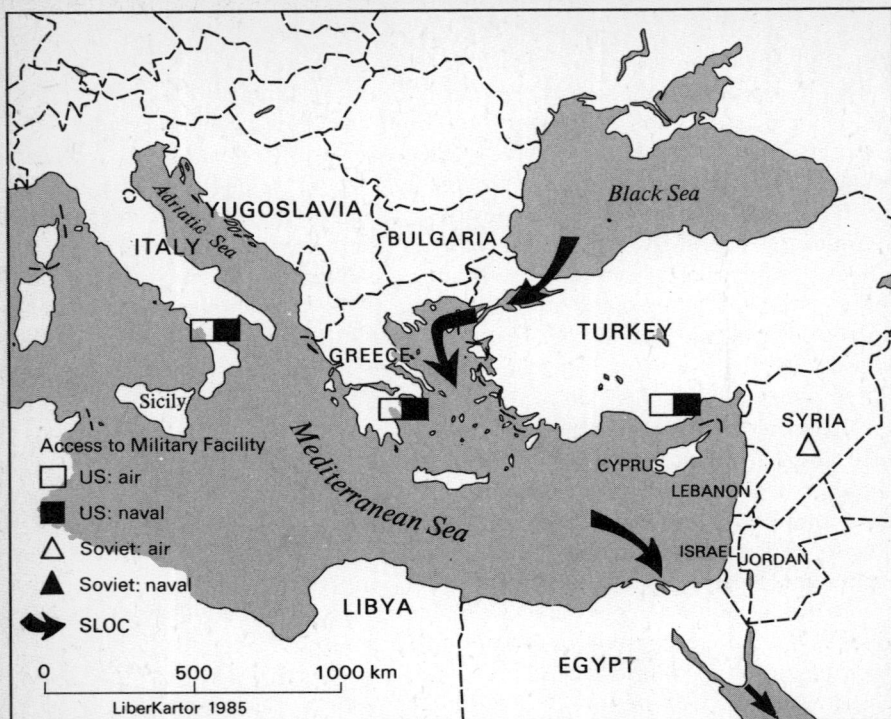

Note: Symbols do not indicate exact locations nor exact numbers of facilities in each country.

Christians and Muslims in Lebanon could also complicate the search for a comprehensive accommodation in the area. The Arab–Israeli conflict is not, of course, the only conceivable source of political instability and tension in the area.

Yugoslavia is also part of the eastern Mediterranean region. (Yugoslavia is, furthermore, a nation that defines itself as a member of the Third World.) While the nation appears to have accomplished its transition to the post-Tito era fairly smoothly, serious divisions remain that could portend future problems. The major, current internal threat is presented by the secessionist movement—associated with sporadic violence—of part of the Albanian minority concentrated in Kosovo province. Visible strains between Serbs and Croatians have lessened since the crisis of the early 1970s but these may flare up again. A prolonged economic recession of the sort the country is currently experiencing could compound problems of internal distribution and exacerbate friction between antagonistic ethnic groupings. A substantial deterioration of the situation in Yugoslavia might create the context for increased Soviet involvement in the country's politics and consequently provide another theatre of US–Soviet competition and tension. There are other issues in the region which could surface. New problems might, for example, be anticipated in Cyprus and the long-term internal stability of Turkey could be questioned.

Compared with the PG/WIO region, the US and Soviet armed presences in the eastern Mediterranean rely somewhat more on arms transfers than on the possession of local military facilities. Following the Camp David Agreement, Egypt has received F-5 fighters from the USA and has ordered F-16s as well. Saudi Arabia, which is proximate to both regions, has been provided with F-15s and promised several AWAC planes. (These are designed for airborne reconnaissance, command and control.) On the other side of the East–West divide, Iraq has received Soviet MiG-21 and MiG-23 aircraft as well as T-62 tanks and Scud missiles. Syria and Libya have acquired MiG-23s and MiG-25s. Each of these nations is among the leading Third World arms importers (table 2).

Table 2. The 10 largest Third World major-weapon importing nations, 1979–83

Importing country	Percentage of total Third World imports
1. Syria	11.8
2. Libya	9.2
3. Iraq	8.9
4. Egypt	7.7
5. Saudi Arabia	7.0
6. India	5.5
7. Israel	4.7
8. Cuba	2.8
9. Argentina	2.8
10. Yemen, South	2.2

Source: SIPRI, *World Armaments and Disarmament, SIPRI Yearbook 1984* (Taylor & Francis, London, 1984), p. 180.

In addition to supplying weapons to local friends and clients, both super-powers have also intervened in the area more directly. In 1980, for example, Moscow and Damascus signed a Treaty of Friendship and Co-operation and more recently, SAM batteries destroyed by Israel have been replaced by more sophisticated Soviet manned SA-5s. Egypt has offered the United States the use of naval facilities at Ras Banas on the Red Sea as well as access to the air base at Cairo West. (It was from here that the aircraft used in the Iranian hostage rescue attempt took off.) Moreover, US troops participated in the multinational force created initially to monitor the Israeli–Egyptian border following Israel's pull-out from Sinai in 1982. The ill-fated international force in Beirut comprised 1 800 US marines as well as French, Italian and British troops. Both US contingents were assigned missions and weaponry of a limited sort but they were not irrelevant to US–Soviet relations in the area. For example, the recent US presence in Beirut and the Soviet presence with the SA-5 batteries in Syria could theoretically have placed US troops within the direct range of Soviet weaponry, thereby increasing the likelihood of a superpower confrontation in the event of a major local conflict (see chapter 4).

Both superpowers maintain substantial naval presences in the Mediterranean. (The US presence includes a Marine Landing Force.) The enmeshing of the two navies necessarily intensifies crisis instability and increases the risk of an armed clash under circumstances of acute regional tension. The US Rapid Deployment Force (USCENTCOM) has the Middle East as well as south-west Asia within its compass. US access to Ras Banas, for example, is designed with this dual mission in mind.[36] Thus, the eastern Mediterranean, like the PG/WIO region, may provide a theatre for future clashes between the two giants. In that eventuality, the numerous nuclear weapons carried by US and Soviet naval forces in these waters would mean that if fighting were to occur, rapid vertical escalation beyond the nuclear threshold would be a real possibility. Other parts of the Third World also form the object of US–Soviet competition but none is as likely to bear as significantly on European security as these two regions.

IV. Other regions

East Asia and the Pacific

Both superpowers have considerable interests in east Asia and the western Pacific. The region has, moreover, witnessed several armed conflicts in which at least one of the two nations has been involved, either directly or indirectly.

US interests in the area are multifaceted. The fact that Japan, Australia and New Zealand are major democracies imparts much symbolic significance to their fate. In addition, the east Asian nations—Japan, South Korea, Hong Kong, Singapore and Taiwan—are among the economically most dynamic countries in the world and are major trading partners of the USA. In fact the volume of US trade with the countries of the region has surpassed that with western Europe.[37] Although the region is known for the vigour of its manufacturing activities, it is also of some importance as a supplier of raw materials. South-east Asia accounts for approximately 80 per cent of world exports of natural rubber. Australia possesses subtantial deposits of bauxite, uranium, titanium and tungsten. Malaysia, Thailand and Indonesia are major sources of US zinc and Thailand also furnishes the US market with columbium and tantalum. (These two metals have applications in jet engines, rockets and missiles.)

The possibility of resource denial is enhanced by the fact that this region also lies astride sealanes of communication of significance to the United States and its regional friends. The Straits of Malacca and Singapore, as well as the Indonesian straits—Lombok, Sunda and Makassar—through which

Figure 3. Superpower access to military facilities in east Asia

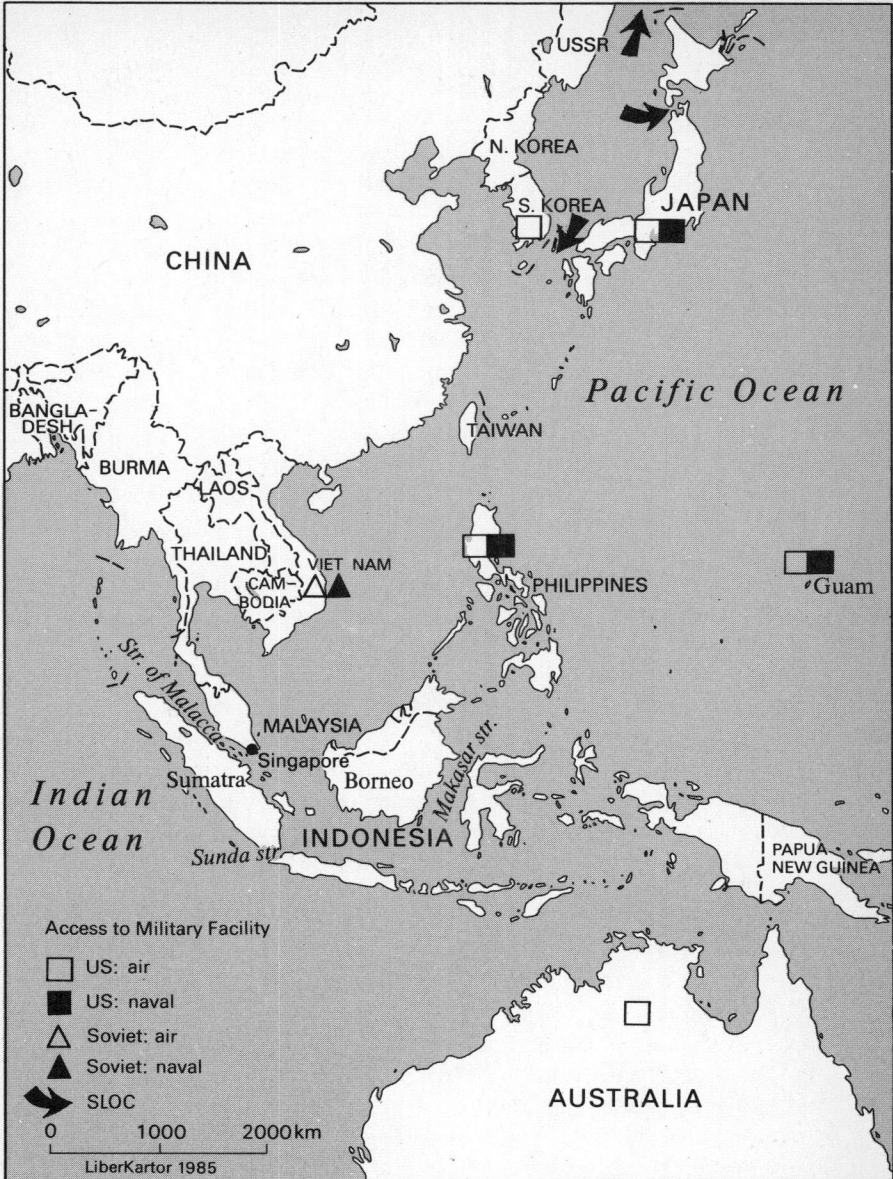

Access to Military Facility

- ☐ US: air
- ■ US: naval
- △ Soviet: air
- ▲ Soviet: naval
- ➤ SLOC

0   1000   2000km

LiberKartor 1985

Note: Symbols do not indicate exact locations nor exact number of facilities in each country.

substantial amounts of petroleum are shipped, are particularly important in this regard.[38]

The USA has important local military installations in the region. The naval base at Subic Bay in the Philippines is one of the most significant US facilities of this sort. Both Australia and Guam host bases for US surveillance flights over the Indian Ocean.[39] The ANZUS treaty formally links the United States to the security of Australia and New Zealand and separate treaties exist with Japan, Thailand and the Philippines. While formally non-aligned, Indonesia's militant anti-Communism makes it a welcome local presence from a US point of view, the more so given Indonesia's recently increased naval and air capabilities.

Although the USSR is presumably not indifferent to the area's economic importance, its local interests are more closely associated with security issues. Approximately one-third of the Soviet submarine force is located in this region, most notably in the Sea of Okhotsk.[40] In addition, Soviet military bases in eastern Siberia and the Kamchatka Peninsula are vulnerable to attacks by US carrier-based aircraft (as well as by F-16s, approximately 40 of which are being deployed on the island of Hokkaido in Japan).

The USA is not the only source of Soviet concern in the region. The Chinese invasion of Viet Nam in 1979 and the continuing strife over Kampuchea maintain Sino-Soviet tension. Japan's growing willingness to increase its military outlays may also worry the Kremlin.

The Soviet Pacific Fleet is the largest Soviet fleet and it benefits from access to the Cam Ranh Bay naval base in Viet Nam. The base is close to the Straits of Malacca, Lombok and Sunda and provides the USSR with a year-round port relatively free of those geographical constraints which limit the usefulness of the Soviet Union's other Asian ports. The US naval presence in the Pacific Ocean is composed of the Third and Seventh Fleets. Both super-powers are currently engaged in substantial shipbuilding programmes that will, in all likelihood, increase their naval deployment in both the Pacific and Indian Oceans. If political tension in the region were to flare up, the enmeshing of the two navies could increase the scope for confrontation —accidental or otherwise—and compound the problems of controlling the crisis with which both sides may be associated. Deployment of dual-capable cruise missiles on naval vessels would clearly increase the dangers.

That the region has a high potential for violence is evident. It is not very likely, though conceivable, that relations between the two Koreas could deteriorate. Although North Korea is not a Soviet ally, active US support of Seoul in a military confrontation between the two Koreas could seem very threatening to Moscow, particularly if such support involved US naval deployments in the vicinity of Vladivostok.

An even greater danger may be rooted in the continuing conflict between the Soviet-supported Vietnamese forces in Kampuchea and the Khmer Rouge backed by the People's Republic of China. It could be difficult to isolate this conflict from its East–West context if US relations with Beijing were to become more intimate or if the conflict spread to Thailand, which is, of course, a US ally. There is, furthermore, some possibility of internal upheaval within nations deemed vital to US security interests. The strong opposition to the Marcos regime in the Philippines and insurgencies in Malaysia and Thailand could, if they were to endanger the security of existing governments, increase US threat perceptions and increase superpower tension in the area.

The Caribbean Basin

Because of its geographical location, the Caribbean Basin is not a part of the world one associates with US–Soviet rivalry. Nevertheless, East–West tension exists there. Since the early 19th century the United States has claimed a proprietary interest in the region.. The region's proximity to the USA—the Gulf Coast is inherently part of the Caribbean Sea—gives it substantial psychological importance. It is feared that a loss of influence within the area would be viewed as a sign of vulnerability. This may account for what would otherwise seem to be astonishingly exaggerated US reactions to political events in the area. Besides this symbolic importance, the area also has geo-political significance.

The Caribbean stretches across vital SLOCs.[41] The Panama Canal links the Atlantic and Pacific Oceans and is thus important both from military and commercial perspectives. In addition, most of the supplies that would be sent to NATO allies in wartime would probably be shipped from US ports in the Gulf of Mexico. Natural resources also make the Caribbean area important to the United States. The Caribbean abuts both Mexico and Venezuela, the two principal suppliers of oil to the USA outside the Persian Gulf. In addition, Jamaica and Venezuela account for nearly half of the USA's bauxite imports.

For reasons of symbolic proximity as well as a real fear of a Soviet regional presence at any level, Washington has always regarded Castro's Cuba as a particularly acute irritant. Nicaragua's move towards the revolutionary end of the political spectrum has caused a reaction whose magnitude is explained by the Reagan Administration's tendency to view all leftward political change in the area as a setback for the USA caused by Soviet machinations. As a consequence, the Cold War has been injected into an area where it might seem to be irrelevant.

The Caribbean Basin may become politically even more explosive than it is now. Extreme economic inequality coupled with harsh dictatorial rule has led to very polarized socio-political systems and to endemic violence in several nations. Ample foundations for political upheaval seem, for example, to exist in Guatemala. Guatemala is contiguous to Mexico and its fate is considered crucial to the USA's own regional position. An escalation of hostilities between Honduras and Nicaragua, particularly if they were to spread to Costa Rica, could raise additional concerns about the security of the Panama Canal.

Figure 4. Superpower access to military facilities in the Caribbean Basin

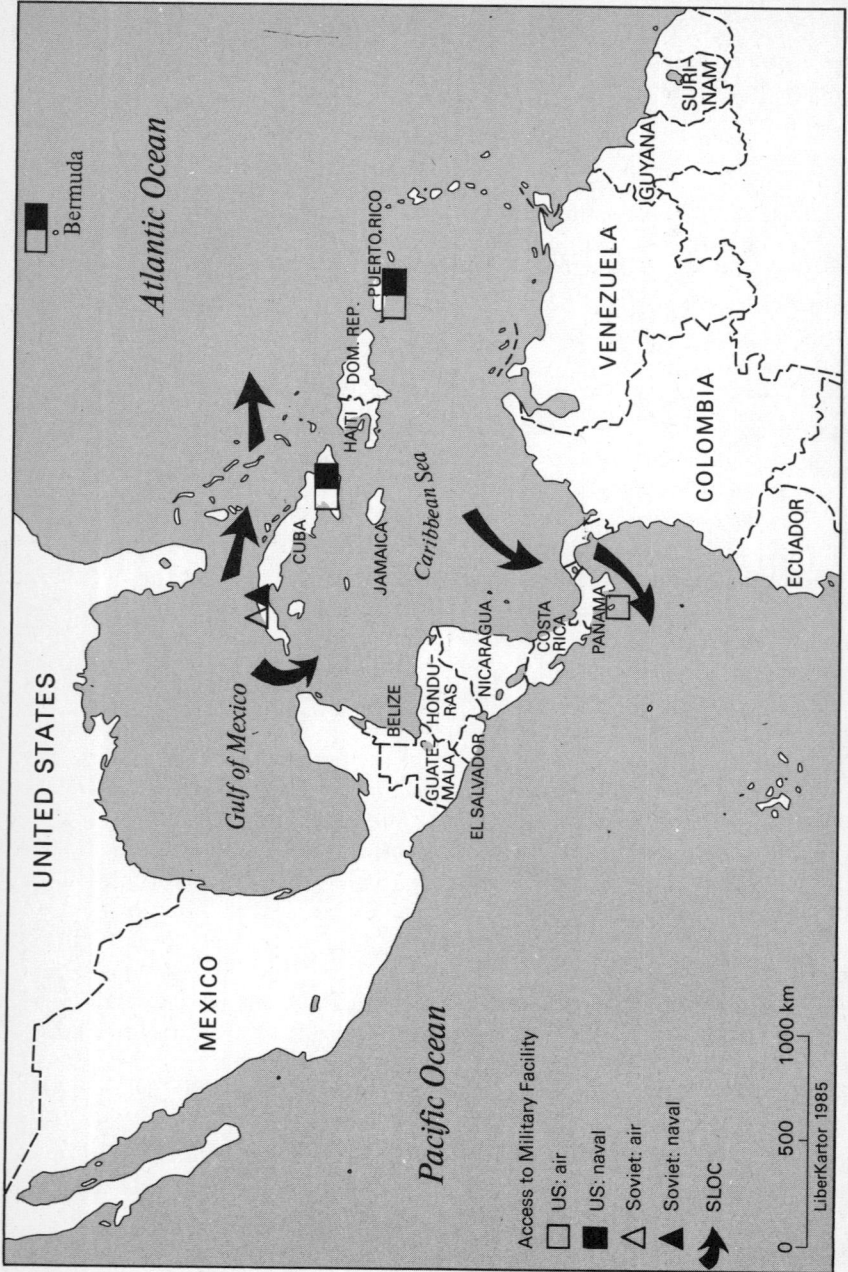

The tone of superpower relations and the current ideological predilections in Washington make it likely that the USA would hold the Soviet Union responsible for perceived threats to US interests in the Caribbean area. An armed confrontation between the two superpowers in the region is clearly very unlikely. But a further deterioration of relations between them over issues originating in the Caribbean, with ramifications spreading to Europe, is entirely conceivable.

V. Conclusion

This chapter has sought to provide a setting in which to assess the consequences for European security of the superpowers' rival entanglements in the Third World. It has surveyed those arenas where the two nations are most likely to clash, particularly the PG/WIO and the eastern Mediterranean, and to a lesser extent, east Asia and the Pacific as well as the Caribbean Basin. The emphasis on the PG/WIO springs from its newly emerging importance to US–Soviet rivalry. The eastern Mediterranean is a highly volatile area too, though this has been apparent for several decades.

The particularities of acute tensions or actual combat in an area will naturally depend on its location. How these tensions affect the security interests of European nations depends on a number of factors. The likelihood and location of superpower regional conflicts are only a part of the relevant context and at least two other kinds of consideration should be kept in mind. One is the nature of the mutual obligations between bloc leaders and their allies. The other is the overall tone of US–Soviet relations.

                  How War Might Spread to Europe

Appendix. Naval nuclear deployments in the Mediterranean area and in the Indian Ocean

	Mediterranean and Black Sea	Indian Ocean
USA		
SSBN	3–4	0
SSN	4–6	2–5
CVN/CV	1–2	1–2
LHA	1	1
Surface combatants	10–12	9–14
USSR		
SSBN/SSB	0	0
SSGN/SSG	2–3	0–1
SSN/SS	10–13	1
Helicopter/VTOL carriers	1–2	0
Surface combatants	7–32	4–5
Patrol craft	0–12	0
CVH9	0	1
UK		
FF	0	1
SSBN	0	0
ASW carriers	0–1	0
Surface combatants	1–2	0
France		
SSBN	0	0
Carriers	1–2	0–1

Source: Arkin, W. M. *et al.*, 'Nuclearization of the oceans', *Symposium on the Denuclearization of the Oceans*, Norrtälje, Sweden, May 1984 (Myrdal Foundation, Stockholm, 1984).

Chapter 3.   Allied dilemmas: dangers of European involvement

I. *Introduction*

If the United States and the Soviet Union did come to blows in those parts of the world where their interests are most likely to collide, how, if at all, could European nations come to be drawn in? An overview of the dangers and possibilities will be provided in this chapter and two specific scenarios will be examined in chapter 4. There is more to be said on this issue from the West European point of view but some observations on the USSR's WTO allies will also be made.

II. *Western Europe*

West European countries could become involved in the Third World duels of the superpowers in three ways: West European countries might participate directly in the military activity as combatants on the side of their bloc leader; they might be less directly involved, providing logistical and other assistance short of actual participation; or they might find themselves involved if either of the superpowers decided to take military operations to European soil in response to a major setback imposed by the other side to its extra-European interests. These three categories are not mutually exclusive; one could lead to another or, indeed, all three could occur simultaneously. The dividing line between the first two forms of participation is, moreoever, often blurred.

Direct participation

The North Atlantic Treaty (article 6) designates its boundaries as comprising the territories of member states, the islands under the jurisdiction of any member in the North Atlantic area north of the Tropic of Cancer and any allied forces, vessels or aircraft in that region or in the Mediterranean. Political and military concerns change, however, and arguments have since been advanced, most notably by the United States, for expanding NATO's role beyond its traditional limits.[42]

A role for NATO

Such arguments have been presented forcefully in recent years; however, history does not seem to favour them. The past few decades have not witnessed a particularly close match between US and European foreign policy objectives in the Third World. For example, the USA has been disinclined to support the colonial and neo-colonial interests of its allies such as in the Suez crisis of 1956. More recently, Western Europe has taken a different view from that of the United States on the Soviet threat in the Third World and on the relevance of East–West antagonisms to North–South relations. US intervention in Viet Nam met with little sympathy and, indeed, frequently with hostility in Western Europe. Sanctions imposed by the USA on the USSR following the invasion of Afghanistan were generally not followed by US allies. US concern with the Soviet role in Angola and the Horn of Africa during the 1970s produced few echoes elsewhere in Europe.

European NATO members have, moreover, traditionally been wary of military commitments outside the continent. They have tended to view the Atlantic Alliance as a *regional* organization designed to secure US commitment to their defence. Suggestions that the treaty's guarantees should be extended, for example, by having its naval mandate cover the South Atlantic, have been resisted. The Scandinavian and Benelux countries in fact questioned, in 1952, the wisdom of bringing Greece and Turkey into the alliance. (Why should they be expected to fight for countries that were geographically so remote?) This resistance has frequently cut across ideological differences. The left has been suspicious that Europe might be drawn into the USA's external military adventures while the right has feared that the US troop presence in Europe might be weakened by extensive commitments elsewhere.

European doubts as to the wisdom of putting too strong a stress on military responses to Third World problems with an East–West dimension are rooted in a different interpretation of the Soviet threat. The Manichean vision which frequently dominates US foreign policy is less characteristic of West European thinking which history has conditioned to view national interests and motivations from more nuanced perspectives. There are also tangible reasons for a greater European inclination to mitigate East–West hostility. To most Europeans, regardless of how they feel about Soviet-type political systems, detente is a desirable and logical arrangement. Although the value of a reasonable degree of military preparedness is generally understood, most governments in the region link their security as much to the relaxation of tensions as to military posture. Because European nations bore the brunt of two world wars, their attitude to detente naturally differs from that of non-European nations.

For certain nations such as the Federal Republic of Germany, the value of improved relations runs deeper still. Major tensions over Berlin have ended with detente. Many families from the two Germanies have been reunited. Visits from west to east have increased considerably.

Economic relations with the Eastern alliance have also expanded appreciably. Exports from Western Europe to the Soviet Union and Eastern Europe increased between 1975 and 1980 from $28.1 billion to $36 billion while imports rose from $16.4 to $41 billion.[43] The Federal Republic of Germany and France account for particularly large shares of the market but several other countries also conduct substantial trade with the Soviet alliance. East–West trade has fallen from its peak in the late 1970s and the Soviet bloc has been forced by circumstances to reduce its imports of manufactured goods from the West by 40 per cent in the early 1980s.[44] But Europe has been alerted to the potential benefits of trade between the two sides, benefits which are mutual and potentially substantial.

To many Europeans it has therefore made no sense to forsake the advantages of detente simply because of Soviet behaviour in the Third World. Yet the possibility of a European entanglement in superpower disputes in the Third World cannot be altogether dismissed. We have identified four areas of the world where Washington and Moscow could conceivably collide. The likelihood of European embroilment will depend on which region is involved. Such involvement is least likely in the Caribbean or east Asia and somewhat more likely in the PG/WIO or the eastern Mediterranean.

Historical associations and commercial relations make Western Europe's interests in east Asia and the western Pacific more substantial than in the Caribbean. Such interests are, nevertheless, limited and the region remains pretty much beyond the reach of European force-projection capabilities. In any case, the USA's NATO allies are not the obvious source of military support for the USA in the area. The major role in this respect would rather devolve upon Japan, Australia and the Philippines. Japan has lately expressed a willingness to expand its military efforts and has been examining ways of playing a greater role, along with the Seventh Fleet, in guarding local sealanes.[45] US logistical installations in Australia and in the Philippines also imply a major role for these two countries in the event of an East–West conflict in the western Pacific. Malaysia and Indonesia would presumably perform significant, though more modest, military functions in such an event. There is thus no reason to expect the European allies to play a major military role in that part of the world. Their participation is far more likely elsewhere, notably in the PG/WIO and the eastern Mediterranean. West European interests are substantial in each of these regions, both of which are within the military reach of at least some of the West European nations.

As table 3 illustrates, the nations of Western Europe are significantly more dependent than the USA on imported oil. They are also much more dependent on the Persian Gulf area for supplies. Some of this oil is shipped by pipeline or via the Suez Canal to the Mediterranean but much of it reaches Europe by the Cape route.

Table 3. Oil dependence of the USA and selected European nations

Country	Percentage of oil imported	Percentage of oil imported from OPEC
United States	21	10.1
United Kingdom[a]	40	15.1
FR Germany	65	38.5
France	82	34.3
Italy	95	54.6

[a]The United Kingdom is a net exporter. In 1982 the UK produced 104 billion tonnes and consumed 77 billion tonnes (*UN Energy Statistics Yearbook 1982*).

Source: Data from *International Energy Statistical Review* (Central Intelligence Agency, Washington, D.C., 30 August 1983).

A disruption in the production or delivery of Persian Gulf oil could critically impair the functioning of West European economies; far more so even than in the case of the USA. Europe also exhibits a reliance on South Africa for many critical minerals. This mineral reliance is comparable to that of the USA (see table 4). European dependence on resources from the two regions is thus substantial and the relative proximity of the regions gives them considerable geostrategic significance.

Table 4. Mineral dependence of the USA and the European Community on South Africa

Mineral	Imports as a percentage of consumption		Percentage of imports from South Africa	
	USA	EEC	USA	EEC
Chrome	90	85	47	50
Vanadium	19	98	45	25
Platinum	85	90	66	28
Cobalt	91	100	..	..
Manganese	98	100	33	45

.. = figures not available

Source: US Department of Defense, *Report of the Secretary of Defense Caspar W. Weinberger to the Congress, Fiscal Year 1985* (US Government Printing Office, Washington, D.C., 1984), p. 96; and *US Mineral Dependence on South Africa*, Committee on Foreign Relations, US Senate (US Government Printing Office, Washington, D.C., 1982).

While the Mediterranean is subsumed within NATO's sphere of responsibility, European members of the Alliance have generally rejected the idea of committing themselves to military intervention in the PG/WIO. There have been instances of symbolic co-operation, as when an informal flotilla with US, French, British and Australian naval forces was assembled near the Persian Gulf at the time of the Iranian hostage crisis in the fall of 1980, or more recently in the context of joint mine-sweeping activities in the Red Sea in 1984. But examples of this sort are rare and most European nations have shown a distaste for such operations. The United States has, on occasion, pressed the point. During Caspar Weinberger's visit to NATO in May 1981, for example, it was reported that he would request co-operation in the form of an international strike force for use in these areas. The proposal appears not to have generated any enthusiasm.[46] Hans Apel, then the FRG Minister of Defence, declared in February 1981 that "expanding the NATO area is out of the question". Even Secretary General Luns has maintained that extending the alliance would "dangerously weaken" it.[47]

European interests in the PG/WIO are considerable and rejecting a military role for NATO as such does not mean that *individual* members would not participate in military operations in the region. Certain members could be especially inclined to assume a military role beyond the traditional confines of the Atlantic alliance and they might also have the force-projection capabilities to do so. France and the United Kingdom both seem currently to fulfil these conditions.

The cases of France and the United Kingdom

The historical record and the military capacity of France suggest that it is the European nation most likely to intervene in regional conflicts in the Third World when its perceived interests so dictate. France is the only European nation that maintains a permanent naval presence in the Indian Ocean. This force operates out of Djibouti and the island of Mayotte (at the mouth of the Mozambique Channel). It has recently been expanded to between 12 and 20 combat vessels, including an occasional aircraft carrier which is said to be equipped with nuclear-armed Super Etendard aircraft, a destroyer, frigates, patrol boats and a minesweeping capability.[48] France also maintains a strong troop presence in many of its former colonial possessions. There are currently some 4 000 troops stationed in Djibouti as well as two squadrons of Mirage fighters and several thousand men are placed on Réunion off Madagascar's east coast. In addition to a permanent local presence in the region, France has developed a quick reaction force, *force d'action rapide* (FAR), that can be airlifted or sealifted for temporary operation abroad.[49] This force numbers some 21 000 men. Moreover, the French government has been quite willing to use its military power in the Third World, as it has shown for example in Zaire, Chad and the Central Africal Republic. It has been reported that the *force d'action rapide* has undertaken military missions in six African countries since 1976, in some of them on more than one occasion.[50]

These interventions have typically involved former French colonies and have been prompted by a desire to maintain a sphere of influence in those areas. This influence has been associated as much with symbolic as with purely military or even economic goals, though access to raw materials has often played some role and may become a more central consideration in the future, particularly as regards the Persian Gulf and southern Africa. France

Figure 5. British and French access to military facilities in the PG/WIO area

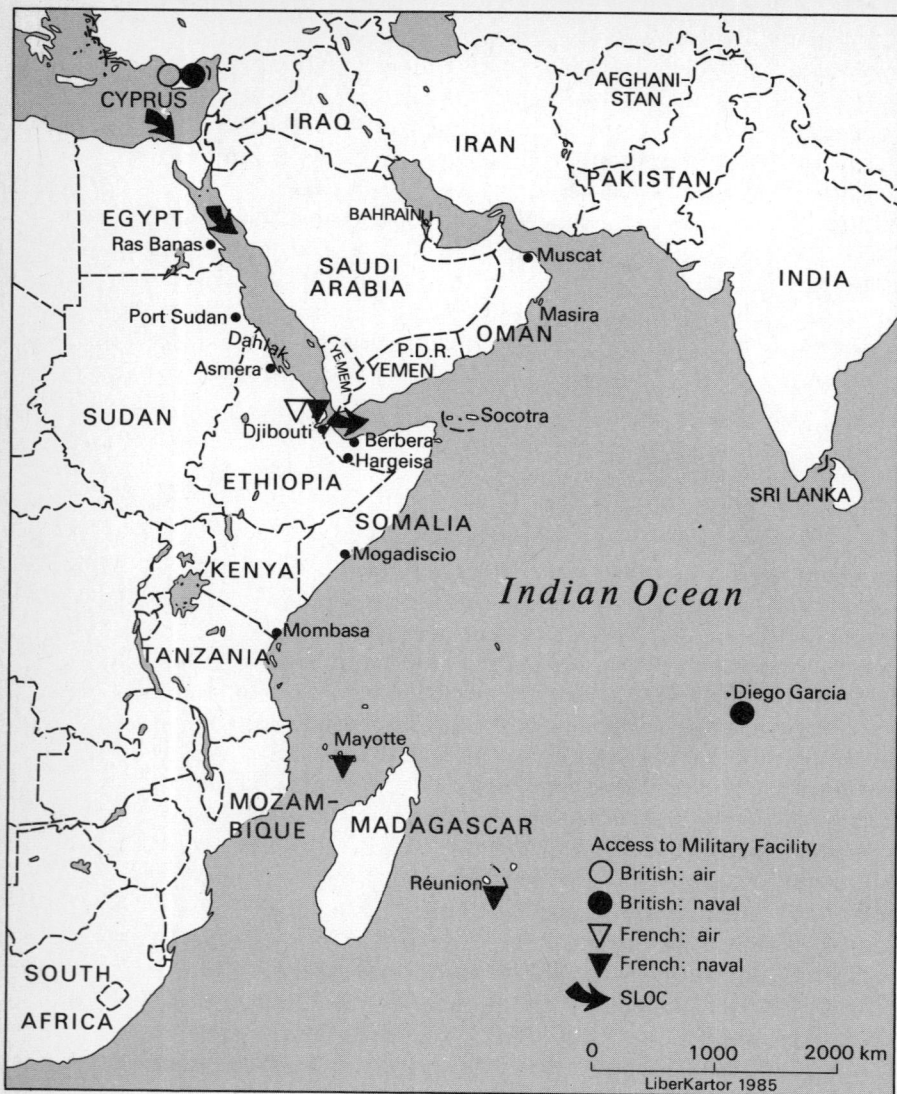

Note: Symbols do not indicate exact locations nor exact numbers of facilities in each country.

depends on the Persian Gulf for a major part of its total oil imports.[51] South Africa and other nations in the vicinity are major sources of the country's raw materials. (French intervention in the Shaba conflict of 1978 in Zaire was probably designed to protect its access to the region's copper mines.) In addition, the Cape Route and the Red Sea Route are two of its major maritime transport lanes.

Although France might well one day intervene in the PG/WIO area, it is by no means certain that this would be at the behest of the USA or even in support of a NATO operation. France is a member of NATO but is not a party to its military structure and its ties to the alliance are looser than those of other members. Furthermore, French foreign policy has always been guided by an exclusively national definition of external interests as was demonstrated, for example, by its attempts to gain preferential treatment from oil-producing states in the mid-1970s. Future external military operations, if undertaken in co-operation with the United States, would probably arise from a temporary coincidence of interests. If, for example, renewed turmoil in the Horn of Africa or conflict in south-eastern Africa were coupled with a Soviet threat to local SLOCs and if this produced an intervention on the part of USCENTCOM, joint naval activity would be conceivable: in the former case in order to secure the Strait of Aden (possibly from Soviet operations launched from facilities in South Yemen); in the latter case to secure the Mozambique Channel (perhaps in a context that included threats from the mainland Mozambique). France would probably wish to avoid a direct engagement with Soviet forces but a clash with Cuban forces or with the forces of Ethiopia, Somalia or Mozambique cannot be ruled out.

The United Kingdom also possesses a capacity for force projection in the Third World. Although the UK does not maintain a significant and permanent naval presence outside the NATO area, it has the ability to dispatch at least a modest naval force far from its shores (as demonstrated in the Falklands/Malvinas conflict) and a naval taskforce goes regularly into the PG/WIO.[52] In a July 1980 white paper on defence the UK expressed an interest in acquiring a broader ability for intervention in the Third World, notably by improving its airlift capacity. The UK maintains hundreds of 'military loan service personnel' in the Persian Gulf region. For example, Oman's air force and navy, which are responsible for patrolling the Straits of Hormuz, rely heavily on seconded UK military personnel. The implications should not be overstated. British armed involvement in the region remains contingent on the unlikely prospect of an oil war and even so would probably be limited in scope. (For example, British troops in Oman could play an advisory role and the naval forces could serve to deter further escalation of the conflict rather than be used for actual combat.)

If France and Britain were to engage in extra-European military action, the present focus of their activities suggests that this would be in different regions. French intervention would probably be directed at Africa while Britain is more likely to find itself engaged in the Persian Gulf. A contribution by either France or the UK to a US effort in the area would probably be the result of bilateral agreements with Washington rather than of express NATO commitments. Political orientation suggests that the UK might more easily find common interests with the United States. The overlap of French and US interests is likely to be rather coincidental (as seen in Chad).

The political circumstances that might precede such interventions remain rather hazy. The situations discussed here are ones which, while possible, are not particularly likely. Should either of the two countries become a direct participant of a superpower conflict within these regions, the consequences for Western Europe would almost certainly go beyond the immediate military costs to France or Britain. Intervention by two NATO members, even outside the institutional context of the Alliance, in a situation of this nature would add a new dimension to the Cold War. It would almost certainly increase the level of threat perception between East and West and would probably extend the militarization of the European continent even after the termination of the extra-regional fighting. The fact that the costs of avoiding such interventions might appear even greater to both Britain and France does not alter the conclusions.

Indirect participation

Allied embroilments in the military disputes of the alliance leaders may assume various forms and need not amount to a direct participation in actual armed conflict with national forces. An ally could, for example, supply weapons or communication facilities to its alliance leader. It might furnish transit facilities for military deliveries to the theatre of combat or provide a staging area from which military operations could be launched. Although the risks inherent in such forms of logistical assistance appear more slight than those stemming from direct military intervention, they may still be substantial. The line between indirect and direct involvement is thin and, initial intentions notwithstanding, easily crossed—frequently because of circumstances that escape the nation's control. This indirect mode of participation in the European conflicts of the United States appears, nevertheless, to have gained the approval of most NATO members.

A division of labour

Transatlantic dialogue on this issue is likely to continue but the current consensus is that while bilateral agreements between the USA and either France or the UK are possible, the responsibility of the European allies is to *facilitate* rather than to participate in US military deployments outside the formal NATO area, particularly in the two regions of special relevance to their own interests. This is to be achieved by a division of labour with two facets. To begin with, the allies would seek to preserve the military balance in Europe if US troops that are normally assigned there but earmarked for the Rapid Deployment Force (USCENTCOM) were dispatched outside Europe. This would require increased defence outlays on the part of other NATO members and such programmes as expanded war-reserve stockpiling. The allies are further called upon to provide logistic assistance for US military activity, particularly in the Persian Gulf and elsewhere in the Indian Ocean. As a NATO communiqué of December 1982 observed: "other individual allied nations, on the basis of national decision, would make an important contribution to the security of the alliance by making available facilities to assist such deployments in such areas".[53] The areas were not explicitly identified but the emphasis seemed to be on the oil-producing regions of the Middle East. While assistance was to be given "on the basis of national decision", the principle seems to be generally accepted within NATO. The concept thus represents a compromise between Washington's desire to have the allies participate actively in its out-of-area ventures and the European preference for avoiding such involvement. It is also an acknowledgement that the members of the Atlantic Alliance have a number of shared interests in economically and strategically vital parts of the world. The vehicle for European assistance for US force-projection objectives is the Host Nation Support (HNS) agreement. One such agreement was signed with the Federal Republic of Germany on 15 April 1982. US Secretary of Defense Weinberger has repeated that: "We continue to make significant progress in developing and expanding wartime HNS agreements with Germany, Belgium, the Netherlands, and the United Kingdom".[54]

The major thrust of the assistance seems to include the provision of *en route* facilities and transit rights for US forces destined for troubled areas. But the record of European support of this type is certainly mixed. During the Six Day War of 1973, for example, all the European NATO members with the exception of Portugal were unwilling to give landing rights to those US aircraft that were airlifting arms to Israel. FR Germany protested at the export of US matériel from US bases in Germany to Israel using Israeli ships.

The USA has nevertheless obtained some future commitments for such assistance and these would presumably be honoured. Specifics would be negotiated on a case-by-case basis with the countries concerned. While the particulars of such agreements are not public knowledge, certain US logistic needs are fairly apparent. Most obviously, in the event of a US intervention in the PG/WIO, troops and military supplies would have to be transported to the theatre of operation from the continental USA. Forces could be dispatched to the Persian Gulf eastwards across the Atlantic or westwards over the Pacific and Indian Oceans. The difference in distance between these two airlanes of communication (ALOCs) is marked: 11 000 kilometres for the eastward route and 19 000 for the westward. A US force using the shorter route would generally require two refuelling stops, one on the west coast of Europe and another in the eastern Mediterranean. Currently this route traces the Azores, Spain, Greece and Egypt.[55]

Certain links in the ALOC chain are particularly important: Portugal's Azores, for example. This archipelago, some 1 600 kilometres west of Lisbon, is a convenient way station for air traffic *en route* to Europe. The Lajes Air Base on the Azores serves as a refuelling facility for US aircraft,[56] particularly C-5A and C-14 transporters headed for European and Mediterranean destinations. (It was clearly essential for the US airlift to Israel in 1973.) The United States is currently upgrading the Lajes facilties.

Within Europe itself, Spain provided the Alliance with access to several military installations even before it joined NATO. The Torrejon Air Base, for example, serves as "a major staging, reinforcement and logistic airlift base for U.S. forces as well as a communications center".[57] In addition, the Rota Naval Base and the air base near Cadiz have provided various relevant services. Despite the usefulness of Spanish bases for US purposes, the unsettled attitude towards the US military presence shown by the Gonzales government may discourage too heavy a reliance on Spain for *en route* facilities and related logistic help. Similar assistance could be obtained elsewhere in Western Europe, notably in the UK, France and Italy.

In the event of a US–Soviet confrontation in the PG/WIO region—most likely in the Persian Gulf itself—or if acute tensions presaged such a confrontation, these allies would be expected to provide overflight and transit privileges. If the assistance did not go beyond this, the direct costs and risks to the nations involved could, but need not, be moderate. The most obvious danger would lie in the possibility of Soviet military action against these countries in order to disrupt shipments or to deter other nations from similarly facilitating the US war effort. But this sort of retaliation may not be very likely since it would require the USSR to intervene against major members of NATO. Such intervention would make it likely that combat would spread to central Europe, bringing with it the possibility of escalation and the prospect of nuclear strikes against the Soviet homeland. Under the circumstances, Moscow would probably seek to confine military activity to the initial theatre—for example, the Persian Gulf or the Horn of Africa— where its geostrategic position is relatively strong rather than expand operations to Europe, even if this meant allowing transit assistance through Europe to continue unhindered. If, however, the USSR did decide to retaliate, there might be no upper ceiling to the conflict (especially since current US doctrine expressly seeks to eliminate gaps in the escalatory ladder).

Greece and Turkey

The situation could be even more precarious if the clash occurred in the eastern Mediterranean where the immediate peril would be greatest for Greece and Turkey. For example, a conflict between Israel and Syria in which Soviet-manned SA-5 rocket installations were attacked could draw the USSR into military action against Israel for the first time. The resulting US–Soviet tension coupled with their respective naval concentrations in the area could then ignite a confrontation between the superpowers. Such a conflict might or might not be terminated at a manageable level, but neither Greece nor Turkey could hope to escape its consequences.

Turkey is a long-standing member of NATO and plays a major role on the southern flank of the Alliance. Turkey might be drawn into a conflict in the eastern Mediterranean but could, in addition, be logistically implicated in

Figure 6.   US access to military facilities in Greece and Turkey

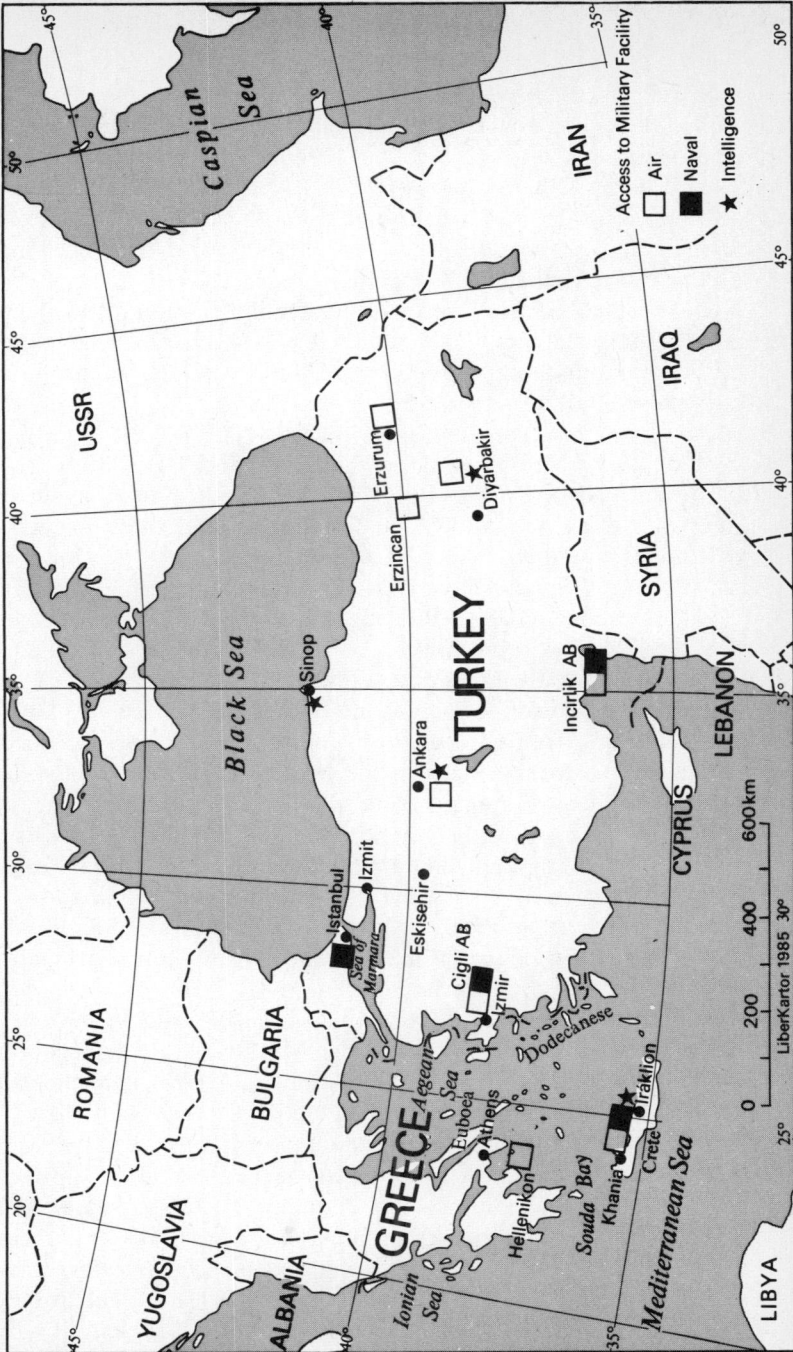

PG/WIO confrontations as well. Efficient Soviet flight routes to the eastern Mediterranean and elsewhere in the Middle East cross Turkish airspace. An airlift of troops and equipment to Syria or, say, Lebanon might require the overflight of Turkish airspace as might an airlift to the Persian Gulf. The Soviet Mediterranean Fleet comes from its Black Sea Fleet. Access to the Mediterranean requires free passage through the Bosporus and the Dardanelles and both of these straits are controlled by Turkey. If attempts were made to bottle up the Soviet fleet by closing these straits Turkey could obviously not remain uninvolved. Turkey, furthermore, has the longest frontier with the USSR of any NATO member.

Turkey's geographical position makes it a valuable location from which to monitor Soviet military activity. The country serves as a forward position for military and information-gathering equipment and could also be useful as a staging area for actual military operations in the area.

The USA maintains a major facility in southern Turkey, the Incirlik Air Base, at which dual-capable fighter aircraft are stationed.[58] The USA also has access to the Ankara Air Station and the Cigli Air Base. An intelligence base at Sinop, near the Black Sea, allows local Soviet naval activity—as well as nuclear tests—to be monitored. The USA operates a long-range radar and communications complex near Diyarbakir and this has assumed particular importance since the loss of US facilities in Iran. There are also 14 Turkish-operated NADGE early-warning radar sites related to the NATO mission.[59] Other facilities are reportedly under development.[60]

The presence on its territory of important facilities used by the USA would make Turkish security extremely precarious in the case of a regional conflict springing, for instance, from a clash in the Middle East. Such installations could presumably serve as staging posts for military forays into the embattled areas if the USA were involved. It may be remembered that the Incirlik Air Base was used in 1958 during the US intervention in Lebanon and in February 1979 during the evacuation of Americans from Iran. Should a conflict directly involve both superpowers, tactical air strikes against the USSR could be launched from Turkey. Pre-emptive or retaliatory Soviet attacks are entirely conceivable under such circumstances (see chaper 4).

The geo-military position of Greece is similarly critical. Greece is strategically located for contingencies in the Middle East and borders on Turkey as well as Yugoslavia, Bulgaria and Albania. The Aegean islands are very important in any effort to control the Soviet Black Sea Fleet. Greece is also crucial to the control of air routes through the region.

The principal military function assigned to Greece is that of supporting operations in the eastern Mediterranean. A major facility is Souda Bay in Crete. It provides a large and convenient anchorage for Sixth Fleet vessels and also has an airfield. Iraklion Air Station provides electronic surveillance of Soviet activities in the area. The USA has used the Hellenikon Air Base —which, like Incirlik in Turkey, was used during the 1979 evacuation from Iran—and has a Fleet Communications System Center at Nea Makri near

Athens. There are also five NADGE early-warning sites throughout Greece.[61] In July 1983 the USA and Greece concluded negotiations allowing the operation of US military bases in Greece for at least an additional five years.

The proximity of Greece to the actual arena of combat, its function as a communications centre and staging post and its role in monitoring Soviet naval and troop movements in the eastern Mediterranean could well make it virtually impossible for Athens to dissociate itself from military operations in this area. Turkey's position could be just as precarious. An assault upon either Turkey or Greece would almost certainly draw in other NATO members in one way or another. The scope of the resulting conflict and the extent of its escalation cannot be confidently anticipated but there is no obvious upper limit to its spread or its destructiveness. The deployment of nuclear-tipped cruise missiles on surface ships in the Mediterranean would be especially threatening, given the present state of military thinking about non-strategic nuclear options (see chapter 1).

Italy

There is at least one additional way in which participation by a NATO member could produce substantial consequences for the rest of Europe as well as for itself. In the controversies surrounding long-range theatre nuclear forces with their emphasis on FR Germany and the United Kingdom, the fact that 112 ground-launched cruise missiles (GLCMs) are to be based in Sicily is sometimes forgotten. The GLCM is a nuclear-tipped vehicle of extreme accuracy with a range of 2 500 km. It is thus well suited to counterforce missions and, based in Sicily, can reach all of the eastern Mediterranean, much of North Africa, the Black Sea, the Persian Gulf and parts of the USSR. The exact targeting structure is not, of course, publicly known but many crucial military installations and forces lie within this area and could be targeted in the event of local conflicts in which the two superpowers oppose each other. Counter-military or even countervalue Soviet retaliation would be entirely conceivable. Specific possibilities will be discussed in the next chapter but it does not require a major feat of imagination to envisage a spread of hostilities to other parts of NATO and WTO territories.

Horizontal escalation

European nations could become implicated in a US–Soviet clash originating in the Third World in yet another way. One superpower might decide to respond to the other's provocation by a countermove against its interests in a different part of the world, possibly in Europe itself. This contingency was raised in connection with the Cuban missile crisis when it was feared that Moscow might move against West Berlin or Turkey if the USA tried to remove the missiles by force. Such a strategy has lately been most clearly advocated by Washington.

Whereas it was previously assumed that force would be countered where it was applied, current thinking is less restrictive. The implications for Europe derive from two explicit assumptions held by the present US Administration. First, the central front in Europe no longer has the exclusive and separate claim to US military concerns that it once appeared to have. It is not a question of fewer resources being devoted to its defence but simply that additional areas are accorded more attention than they once were. As Secretary of Defense Caspar Weinberger has pointed out: "it has become increasingly clear that the members of the Alliance in the northern, center, and southern regions are bound together as one and critically depend on each other and even outside the NATO Treaty boundaries—notably the Persian Gulf".[62]

Second, it is understood that the USA does not enjoy regional military superiority in every part of the world and may not be in a position to deter aggression on every front nor to ward it off should deterrence fail. The comparatively tenuous US position in the Persian Gulf is of particular concern to Washington despite the recent military build-up in the area. In Caspar Weinberger's words:

> We may be forced to cope with Soviet aggression, or Soviet-backed aggression, on several fronts. But even if the enemy attacked at one place *we* [emphasis in original] might choose not to restrict ourselves to meeting aggression on its own immediate front. We might decide to stretch our capabilities, to engage the enemy in many places, or to concentrate our forces and military assets in a few of the most critical arenas.[63]

Thus the possibility of response by horizontal escalation, whereby a Soviet attack in one part of the world would be counteracted by a US military move elsewhere, has been incorporated into Washington's declaratory strategy. But where might such a countermove occur? Specifics are rarely discussed although broad hints are occasionally dropped. In the pages where this doctrine was initially articulated the Secretary of Defense also observed: "Some important Soviet vulnerabilities have to do with the fact that the Soviet empire, unlike our alliance, is not a voluntary association of democratic nations... Our plans for counteroffensive in war can take account of such vulnerabilities on the Soviet side".[64]

Thus it is suggested that the internal integrity of the Soviet alliance could be assaulted in response to a provocation elsewhere, particularly in the Persian Gulf. East European regimes, and possibly societies, would in this scenario be the ultimate victims of the provocation. Clearly the escalatory risks in such a situation are enormous. The cohesion and integrity of the Soviet alliance as a buffer against the West ranks very near the top of the Kremlin's security concerns. From Moscow's perspective there might be virtually no countermove that would appear excessive. And even if both sides sought to control the level of conflict on the central European front, the extreme density of population, the massive concentration of conventional force, the local deployment of tactical and theatre nuclear weapons and the logic of decision-making under conditions of actual combat would make the nuclear devastation of both Europe and the superpowers a very likely outcome.

The enormous risks associated with military action in this part of the world make one wonder just how seriously the Secretary of Defense's statement about Eastern Europe should be taken. Given the extreme sensitivity of this issue from a Soviet point of view, the *threat* could have a powerful deterrent effect on any project the Kremlin might entertain with regard to the USA's extra-European interests. But the formidable danger of uncontrollable escalation makes it unlikely that the threat would really be acted upon should deterrence fail. In other words, the USSR might be too averse to the risk to test US resolve on this issue but if it were to do so the USA would probably be too prudent to carry out its declaratory strategy.

There are, however, other more suitable places for a counter-offensive. One possibility is Cuba. The Castro regime has been a thorn in the side of the USA to an extent quite disproportionate to its actual ability to jeopardize fundamental US interests. A successful US invasion could be carried out with relative ease and while the risks of all-out escalation are real they might not be inordinately high. Nevertheless, there are not many situations where an attack on Cuba would be the anticipated counter-response of the USA. For despite its symbolic value and occasional military usefulness to the Soviet Union, Cuba is not really a major political or geostrategic asset. An assault on Cuba would not, in most circumstances, fulfil the condition that "it should be launched against territory or assets that are of an importance to [the enemy] comparable to the ones he is attacking".[65]

Soviet interests in east or south-east Asia represent another possible target for a counter-offensive. The region is important to Soviet security and could thus commend itself in a way that Cuba does not. Naval action against Soviet SLOCs in the area would be feasible as would, for example, an attack on Viet Nam with the support of regional US allies. This could deprive the USSR of an important outpost and of access to the warm-water port of Can Rahn Bay. The same end might be achieved without an all-out US invasion, for an attack on Vietnamese armed forces of sufficient strength could open the door to a Chinese invasion and occupation. This part of the world thus presents real possibilities for retaliation but the impact on the European nations would be quite indirect. The overall level of East–West tension would surely be raised and the conflict might eventually spread as far as Europe. But the most pressing question for this study is: where, if anywhere, could a US counter-offensive occur in Europe?

There are two essential properties which an area must have in order to qualify. First, its importance to the two superpowers must be such that a successful US assault would offset even a major Soviet gain in the Third World. Second, the area must be such that it is possible to control the *vertical* escalation of the conflict because no actual counter-offensive, as opposed to the mere threat, is presumably worth a serious likelihood of nuclear devastation wrought on the USA. On this basis, the seas abutting Norway must be considered a likely arena for horizontal escalation.

The USSR has a substantial military interest in this region and the US hand would be considerably strengthened by control of these waters. The Norwegian and Barents Seas host a major portion of the Soviet submarine fleet based in Murmansk on the Kola Peninsula. Some two-thirds of the Soviet Union's nuclear missile-bearing submarines (SSBNs), protected by approximately the same fraction of its nuclear attack submarines (SSNs) and probably a quarter of its naval surface combatants and naval aviation capabilities are based on Kola.[66]

Two sorts of mission could be launched from this location. First, the Soviet Union could move to interdict SLOCs in the North Atlantic through which US reinforcements would be sent to the European allies in the event of a conventional conflict. The ability to provide continuous reinforcements has acquired special relevance in view of the Reagan Administration's belief in the possibility of protracted conventional warfare. Consequently, offensive action against the Soviet submarine fleet might be undertaken in retaliation for an extra-European provocation and the full range of US anti-submarine warfare (ASW) capabilities deployed in the northern seas might be applied to this end. The prize could be the future security of US SLOCs in the north Atlantic.

Second, and perhaps more importantly, it is from the Norwegian and Barents Seas that the USSR might launch its strategic submarine-launched ballistic missiles (SLBMs) in the event of a duel between Soviet and US central strategic systems. Destroying the Soviet ballistic missile-equipped, nuclear-powered submarines (SSBNs) before these can launch their missiles would be a major gain to the USA and a correspondingly significant loss to the Soviet Union. The progress in Soviet strategic submarine capability has enhanced the significance of such a mission.

Until recent years, Yankee-Class submarines were the dominant component of the Soviet SSBN fleet. These submarines were equipped with SS-N-6 or SS-N-17 missiles which, if fired from the Barents Sea or the northern Norwegian Sea, lacked the range to reach the USA. In order to come within reach of targets in the USA the submarines were obliged to pass through two major choke-points. The first of these is located between the Norwegian mainland and Bear Island (see figure 7) and lies across the sealane leading from the Barents Sea into the Norwegian Sea. The second and better-known of the two choke-points is the Greenland–Iceland–United Kingdom (GIUK) gap. Both gaps are presumably well furnished with the full gamut of submarine-detection devices and ASW weaponry. Soviet submarines could thus have been attacked at the point of transit into the Norwegian Sea and the North Atlantic at choke-points where they would be at a definite disadvantage.

The Soviet submarine force has since made considerable strides. The SS-N-

Figure 7. The northern flank

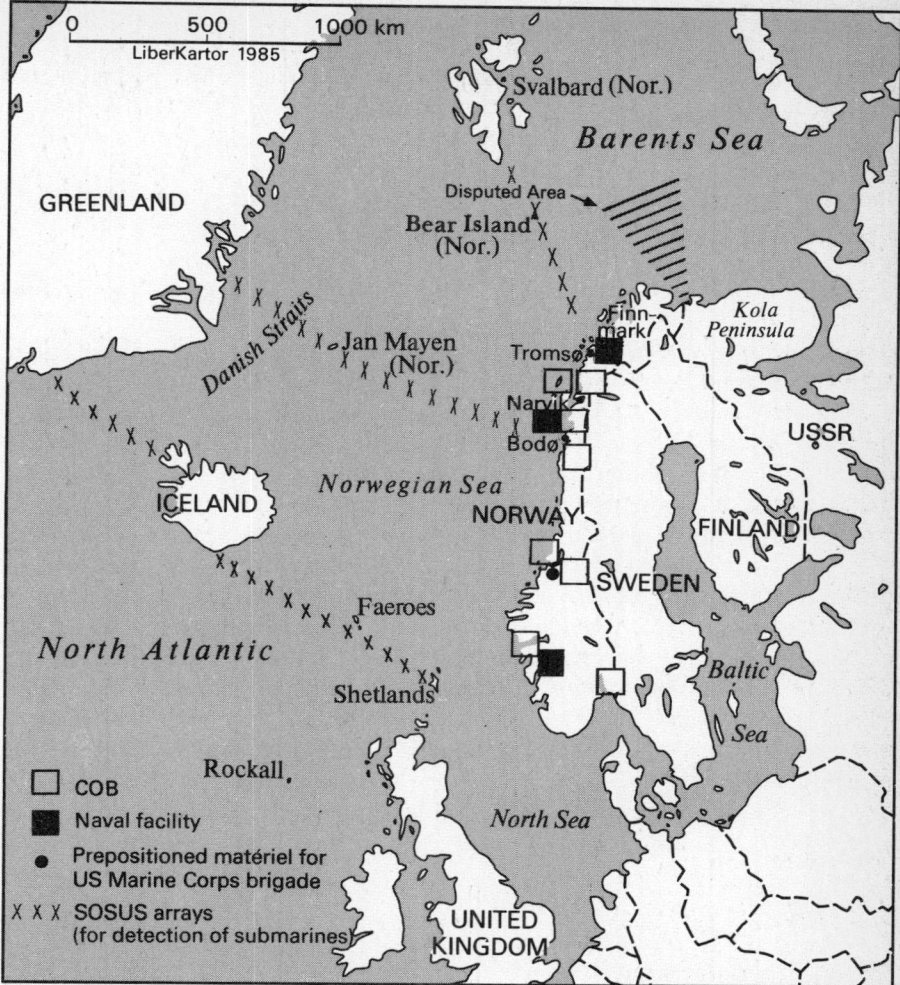

8 SLBM with a range of 7 700 kilometres was introduced on the newer Delta-Class submarines in the early 1970s. More recently, two Typhoon-Class submarines have been launched—one deployed in northern waters—armed with the even longer-range SS-NX-20 missiles. All of North America is apparently within range of this latter type. The implication is that a growing proportion of Soviet SLBMs can be fired from home waters and need not, therefore, brave the choke-points. Conversely, if the USA wish to challenge or to incapacitate the Soviet SSBN fleet it would have to carry its ASW attacks directly into northern or Soviet waters. As Steven Miller points out: "whereas before NATO's aim was simply to deny Soviet forces free access to

the North Atlantic, now it must be concerned about fighting its way into the Norwegian Sea".[67]

There are two major ways in which the USA could stand to gain, and the USSR to lose, by a successful offensive action against Soviet submarines in this area. Navy Secretary John Lehman has been very frank on this score: "with regard to Europe, for instance, why should we stay south of the GIUK gap... Why should we stay in a pulled-back defensive maritime strategy: when the payoff of going north of the GIUK gap and going after [the Soviets] and their interdiction capabilities is so high; and where geography is really on our side . . .?"[68]

In sum, the Soviet submarine fleet north of the GIUK gap is rightly considered a formidable prize, one that could be viewed as a substantial compensation for even a major loss in the Third World. Moreover, in accordance with our second major qualification for a plausible locus of retaliation, it appears that such a counter-offensive need not create a very high risk of nuclear warfare. For while the strategic significance of the Soviet SSBN fleet in the northern sea is great, it is not of the same order of magnitude as the maintenance of obedient buffer states on its western borders. Thus, rightly or wrongly, it might be judged that even such high stakes would not be worth actual nuclear conflict in the eyes of the Kremlin. Moreover, the risks of collateral damage in a battle of the Norwegian Sea might, unlike the case of the central front, seem slight. After all, how much civilian destruction could combat beneath the surface of the sea within the Arctic Circle cause? The escalatory pressures that would be produced by combat in densely populated central Europe would, it appears, be virtually absent here. The credibility of these assumptions will be discussed in the following chapter but on the basis of what has been said so far it must be concluded that the idea of a US counter-offensive in this part of the world is not entirely fanciful.

III. Eastern Europe

We have dwelt at some length on the circumstances that could lead the USA's West European allies to become involved in US confrontations with the Soviet Union in the Third World. But what of the other side of the Cold War divide? What can be said about the possibility of the USSR's WTO allies finding themselves entangled in such conflicts?

We have examined three roads that could lead to US allied involvement in extra-European superpower conflicts. The same scheme can, in principle, be applied to the Soviet alliance. Direct military involvement at any significant level by the WTO allies in Soviet Third World ventures would seem unlikely. Soviet foreign policy calculations as well as the interests of the Soviet Union's European allies make this a very remote contingency. Past instances of such participation can admittedly be found but are both scarce and of marginal significance.

Military technicians from WTO allies have assisted the Soviet Union's clients and friends in the Third World. The GDR has played an especially active role in this respect. Military advisers from the GDR were present in Ethiopia in 1978 during the conflict with Somalia and in 1981 it was estimated that 180 military personnel from the German Democratic Republic were still present in Ethiopia.[69] East German soldiers and military advisers have also been shipped to Angola where they apparently helped to build up the national air force as well as a paratroop division and also trained Angolan soldiers and militia.[70] Some 1 000 East Germans were thought to have still been there in 1981. In late 1977 the Western Somali Liberation Front claimed to have taken prisoner "seven Russians, three Bulgarians, and two East Germans".

Moscow, like Washington, has occasionally expressed a desire to have its allies play a more active role in extra-European theatres. For example, General Aleksei A. Yephishov, Chief of the Political Department of the Soviet Armed Forces, stated in 1980 that other members of the WTO would also stand ready to guarantee the security of fraternal Marxist nations such as Afghanistan. According to Yephishev: "The joint power of the countries of the Socialist community embodied in the Warsaw Pact organization serves [as] a dependable guarantee of nations building a new life".[71]

East European activity in this regard has nevertheless been limited. Although the GDR's combat role remains unclear, there is every indication that the presence of the Soviet Union's other WTO allies in the Third World has been of an advisory, non-combatant sort. These countries have, in fact, been traditionally disinclined to get too deeply entangled in the Soviet Union's non-European problems as evidenced by the Sino-Soviet rivalry. At the time of the border clashes of 1969 the Kremlin pressed for collective defence in the east, but it won almost no support for this concept among its allies.[72] This reticence has extended to their avoiding a strong position on such issues as the conflict between Viet Nam and Kampuchea or even the Camp David agreement. With the exception of Romania the WTO countries accept the notion of coalition warfare which implies that their forces would participate alongside those of the USSR in rapid operations against NATO. But they have stayed aloof from their alliance leader's global military concerns by resisting, for instance, the incorporation of non-European Marxist nations into the WTO, or the stationing of even token contingents along the Sino-Soviet border.

In any case, it is unlikely that the USSR would hazard injecting East European forces into Third World conflicts. For one thing this would weaken the USSR's military position in Europe and Soviet strength on the continent would almost certainly be Moscow's primary concern. Second, if armed conflict with the West were to erupt or seemed imminent, the Kremlin would probably be worried about the danger of unrest *within* the Alliance and would not wish to send elsewhere the allied national troops that might be needed to quell internal disturbances. (Such disturbances could easily assume an anti-Soviet character.) A final and important point is that the reliability of allied troops sent to intervene in, say, the Persian Gulf or West Africa would be open to doubt.[73] The loyalty of national military elites could not be confidently assumed in the cases of Hungary, Czechoslovakia or Poland, and a forced foreign intervention might lead to further misgivings about the alliance link. Hungary and Czechoslovakia have both had to countenance Soviet armed invasions and some residual resentment within the military establishments may be expected. Moreover, developments in Poland over the last few years substantially limit that country's role as a military partner. Romania, despite its WTO membership, has identified national territorial defence as the only legitimate function for its armed forces and would be a higly implausible participant in Soviet armed adventures abroad. It appears that the Soviet Union only has real confidence in the military establishments of the GDR and Bulgaria. Yet even this loyalty might not be sustained in the face of a major military entanglement involving significant risks and costs. Although the military elites themselves might be willing to act at the Kremlin's behest, it is not likely that the people of either country would identify closely with Soviet interests in the Third World. Their resentment could well be aroused by the sacrifices suffered for the sake of these interests. Some rancour could certainly be expected on the part of the East German public if the scope of the participation was large and the political costs to the USSR might soon outweigh whatever benefits might be derived from the ally's military support.

An alternative strategy has, in fact, been open to the Soviet Union. Cuban forces participated actively in the Angolan Civil War in 1975 and were instrumental in fending off armed assaults by South Africa and Zaire. Cuban forces have also bolstered the position of Agostino Neto's MPLA against its FNLA and UNITA opponents.[74] At peak strength, Cuba's expeditionary force was estimated at 36 000 men. In late 1977, in response to a request by Ethiopia's leader Haile Mengistu, Cuban combat troops were again dispatched to Africa in order to assist in the conflict with Somalia over the disputed Ogaden region. Havana's military advisers also appear to have been sent to South Yemen and to Equatorial Guinea.

Cuban action was probably not just a result of Soviet directives. Revolutionary internationalism as well as a romantic ethnic identification with Africa—the majority of Cuba's population is either black or mulatto —may have been the major reasons for providing military assistance to African nations. But these interventions have certainly dovetailed with Soviet interests. Moscow had supported the MPLA for several years before Angola's independence and was also the first nation to recognize Neto's People's Republic of Angola when it was first proclaimed in November 1975. The Soviet Union had similarly supported Ethiopia against Somalia from 1976 and had been Mengistu's major source of arms. Cuban troops benefited from Soviet airlifts in both Angola and Ethiopia and also, in the case of Angola, from Soviet sea transportation.

Direct participation by the Soviet Union's East European allies in armed activities in other parts of the world appears decidedly unlikely. Such participation would carry substantial costs, would hold out few benefits to these countries and would, in addition, involve major risks for the Soviet Union's political and military position in Europe.

Even an *indirect* involvement of the WTO countries in such conflicts appears implausible. Unlike Britain and France, no East European nation has military installations in the Third World nor does any of them have a significant force-projection capacity that could be put into Soviet service. A major form of indirect support by the USA's NATO allies would be the provision of overflight rights and *en route* facilities for the shipment of US troops and supplies to theatres of operation in the Third World. By contrast, the very proximity of the USSR to such theatres means that the WTO allies are not likely to be called upon for this sort of assistance, particularly since, with the possible exception of Bulgaria, they do not lie within the relevant geographical paths.

Soviet intervention in the Persian Gulf—in itself an implausible contingency—would probably involve airborne divisions dispatched from Kirovabad in Georgia and Fergana in Turkestan.[75] In neither case would it be necessary to overfly any East European nation. If the military operation were to occur in the Horn of Africa, the situation might, but would not need to be, different. The airlift of Soviet supplies to Ethiopia during the latter's conflict with Somalia relied at one stage on aircraft that departed from Black Sea bases and flew to Addis Ababa across Bulgaria and Yugoslavia via Libya and Sudan. This was not, in fact, the only possible route and from December 1977 onwards most flights traversed the Middle East on their way to Ethiopia.[76] Bulgaria's participation also included the maritime transport of supplies to the ports of Massawa and Assab via the Bosphorus and the Suez Canal. This was only a marginal role and not one that could easily be expanded.

On the whole, the Soviet Union's WTO allies have less logistic relevance to its military needs in the Third World than do several NATO members for the USA. Since direct participation by East European troops in such conflicts is highly improbable, the implications of superpower disputes and possible armed confrontation in the Third World on other WTO members are less immediate and obvious than in the case of the Atlantic alliance.

IV. Summary

We have looked into the conditions that could cause European nations to become embroiled in the extra-European military conflicts of their alliance leaders and we have drawn mixed conclusions. NATO countries have, as a rule, resisted extending the responsibilities of the Alliance beyond its traditional confines and have typically spurned US attempts to engage them in its military presence in the Third World. Both France and the United Kingdom could, on the basis of national decisions, assume some external military role in the PG/WIO. For France this would probably be on the east coast of Africa and for the UK in the Persian Gulf. Such a course could, but need not, involve a military clash with Soviet forces. Even if this were avoided, there would be serious and enduring consequences for East–West relations in general, including substantially heightened tensions and increased militarization of the European continent. Britain and France might, initially, perceive this prospect as being less immediate and tangible than the costs of not acting. The need to make a choice of this sort would reflect a failure of overall security policy which should be designed to make such choices unnecessary.

Indirect modes of West European participation in the superpowers' conflicts would include, most obviously, the provision of *en route* assistance and other forms of logistic succour to the USA for its military operations in the Third World and, under the emerging concept of 'division of labour', within NATO. Again, the immediate military consequences could be limited but, as in the previous case, ultimate European security could be the main victim. The indicated conclusion is, once again, that policy should be directed to forestalling such predicaments.

The major military risk is that a conflict in the eastern Mediterranean, most probably one erupting in the Middle East, could come to involve both the Soviet Union and the United States. Given the crucial logistic function that Turkey and Greece would be called upon to play, an initially indirect role could rapidly escalate to direct military participation. Under such circumstances, it is entirely conceivable that the conflict might spread to other parts of Europe. Horizontal escalation of hostilities could bring an extra-European conflict to other parts of the world, possibly the NATO northern flank.

The USSR's WTO allies, for their part, appear less central to Moscow's needs and objectives in the Third World. The Soviet Union would almost certainly find it unwise to implicate its East European allies in its own military ventures outside Europe, although their *symbolic* participation could be deemed useful to legitimize Moscow's own policies. The Soviet Union's WTO allies have generally resisted any extra-European military role. The exceptions so far have been the GDR and, to a lesser extent, Bulgaria. Their contribution to the Soviet goals has, however, been modest and both countries would find it difficult to extend their involvement. Also, the Soviet Union's WTO allies do not have much of an indirect, logistic role to play in most plausible scenarios of military operations in the Third World. An extension of actual armed conflict to European territory would certainly involve Soviet allies. Most other contingencies would rather affect them, as they would most NATO members, by their broad and lasting implications for East–West, and hence intra-European, relations.

Chapter 4.   Two scenarios

I. Introduction

The previous chapter provided a broad overview of the ways in which out-of-area superpower conflicts could impinge upon the security of the superpowers' European allies. It described the general outlines of the situation but did not speculate on concrete sequences of moves and countermoves which could cause the European countries to be drawn into such confrontations. A more specific treatment may be useful and some explicit scenarios will therefore be examined.

Such an exercise may generate several benefits. The basic parameters of the situation—the external interests, force postures and declaratory strategies and policies—merely provide the framework within which horizontal and vertical escalation could occur. It is the specific political and military decisions that define the actual nature of the escalation. Policy recommendations will thus be most useful if they are simultaneously cast at two levels: one level designed to affect the structure of the situation and the other aimed at the actual decisions that are part of any escalatory sequence. These decisions can merely be guessed at and it is the function of scenarios to attempt this.

The inherent limitations of scenarios should be recognized. No claim can be made to prophetic insight into future crises and outlining a scenario is bound to involve a degree of speculation and simplification which inevitably produces some discrepancy with reality. The best that can probably be done is to select a maximally plausible set of assumptions and to apply common sense to the pursuit of their implications. Competing assumptions appear at each stage of the scenario's unfolding and a good deal of subjective judgement necessarily enters into the business of choosing among them. The number of causal sequences that can be considered must, moreover, be restricted from the beginning. Each branch spawns new branches and their profusion at any stage of the scenario is exponentially related to the number of possibilities allowed at an earlier stage. A manageable story must, of necessity, be rather a simplified story. But these limitations do not mean that, in their essentials, scenarios are necessarily ill-matched to future events.

The fact that a good scenario is simplified and stylized should only mean that less important or less likely contingencies have been recognized and omitted. There is, moreover, a substantial heuristic utility in the exercise itself, for the task of explicitly stating assumptions and drawing their implications, and the need to repeat this exercise through several rounds of anticipatory reasoning, lays these assumptions and inferences open to scrutiny and challenge. Of the numerous possible sources of crisis outlined in chapter 3, there are two that would seem most likely to erupt and which would have the greatest consequences: turmoil in the Persian Gulf or a renewed Arab–Israeli conflict.

II. *The Persian Gulf*

A frequent—though sometimes implicit—assumption concerning the Persian Gulf region is that the USSR might decide to exploit the improved geo-strategic situation which it has enjoyed since the invasion of Afghanistan and make a military move into the Gulf area. It would thus ensure its own petroleum needs, impose a stranglehold on the oil-dependent Western economies and put itself in a position to threaten Indian Ocean SLOCs. A similar, though reversed, interpretation might be applied by the Kremlin to the expanded US military presence in the area. On the whole though, scenarios that assume outright invasions are implausible. A major crisis in the Persian Gulf is not likely to stem from a decision by either superpower to secure its interests in this fashion. The USA would have much to lose and little to gain. The USSR would stand to gain substantially, but the costs and risks involved would be enormous. While Moscow has been willing to use force against its neighbours in order to avoid losing what it has already acquired—as in Hungary, Czechoslovakia and Afghanistan—it has not engaged in such actions with a view to making *new* gains and has, on the whole, avoided ventures with a significant military risk.[77]

To the extent that direct military entanglement in the region on the part of the superpowers (and possibly of their allies) actually occurs, it is likely to follow a multi-stage process of progressively deeper engagement. Furthermore, the greatest threat to their interests, or the most obvious opportunity for new gains, is likely to come from the eroding internal situation of a Persian Gulf nation in which the two sides have a substantial stake. Such a country would be one whose oil wealth and/or geostrategic location was such that a change of loyalties could decisively reverse the regional balance towards one or other superpower.

Which nations fulfil these criteria? The Persian Gulf nations of greatest importance to the economic and security calculations of the superpowers are Saudi Arabia, Iran, Iraq and Oman. Though not actually a Gulf nation, Pakistan with its landmass and its port of Karachi is immediately contiguous to the area and, by stretching the concept a little, may be considered part of this region as well. (It is, in any case, within the area which USCENTCOM is considered to encompass.) Every one of these countries is of the utmost importance to both superpowers, and each contains the seeds of domestic turmoil and of powerful centrifugal forces. A brief survey of their domestic political situations may be helpful.

In Pakistan the major threat comes from the numerous separatist guerrilla campaigns which have been active since the early 1970s. Restive ethnic groups include the Sindhi and Pushtan minorities, but the most powerful challenge comes from Baluchi separatism in western Pakistan. The Zia regime has encountered other sorts of resistance as well, resistance which seems to be dealt with by widespread incarceration and execution. But though it has many facets, the opposition does not appear to have attained widespread support and by the standards of many Third World countries, the regime's position is probably not too precarious. Given the structure of much of the non-ethnic opposition, it seems that if the regime does nevertheless collapse, this might be caused by a forced return to the Western-style democracy that existed before Zia's 1977 take-over.

In Iraq, a major threat to Sadam Hussein's regime comes from the armed struggle for autonomy waged by the Kurds. The Kurds have been aided by Iran and, apparently, by Syria as well. A coalition of Kurds from Iraq, Iran and Syria—as well as of dissident Iraqi Shiites, Ba'athists and army officers—has, in fact, been created in opposition to Hussein. But the regime seems to be pretty much in control at the moment and, anyway, it is unlikely that such a disparate coalition will stick together for long, or that any of its parts will manage to increase its support significantly in the near future. Ultimately its political future may be determined by the course and costs of the Iran–Iraq war. The regime is challenged but is not, as yet, seriously imperilled.

There are several sources of instability within Saudi Arabia. Individually none of these sources is particularly strong, but their aggregate weight could be significant. Here too, it is not very probable that the opposition will generate much support during the next 5–10 years. There is indeed some religious opposition and this could have significance since the House of Saud derives its legitimacy from its Unitarian (Wahhabi) Islamic base (and the Koran remains the country's constitution). But the size of this opposition seems to be quite modest. The seizure of the Grand Mosque by funda-mentalist religious zealots in November 1979 did generate speculation about the firmness of the regime's source of legitimacy but the overall impression was that the attackers represented no significant domestic constituency and that the whole affair was an isolated incident.

There may be other sources of opposition but none that is really substan-tial. The middle class has seen its status increase with the oil-induced surge in economic growth but has been granted virtually no role in the country's political life. It seems, however, to be content with its financial position and not to be actively seeking an expanded role in politics. Military opposition cannot be dismissed either, since there have been instances—mainly involving the air force—of discontent in the armed forces. But here again, examples of this sort seem disconnected and there have been no indications of an overall military plot to unseat the House of Saud.[78] Given the formidable regional asset that Saudi Arabia would represent to the Soviet Union, a real threat to the regime's security would be an extremely grave matter from the US point of view. But such a threat is not on the immediate horizon and is, in any case, not the major threat to regional stability.

In Oman, Sultan Qabus appears to be firmly in control of his nation. Challenges from Dhofar rebels some years ago were successfully repressed and the Sultan's security forces appear quite loyal. One source of instability may prove to be the rapidly growing number of people with secondary school or higher education and ways will have to be found of absorbing them satisfactorily into the economy. This ought not, however, to be an insuperable problem.

Of the nations surveyed here, Iran with its internal situation may prove to be the most explosive in the future. The personality of its current leader with his quasi-mystical authority and harsh dictatorial rule and the state of active belligerence with Iraq have managed to mute the numerous sources of intense discontent. But the situation may well change in the near future. Ethnic strife is a dominant feature of the Iranian political scene. The most active and powerful separatist groups are the Kurds and the Baluchis. Both have waged sporadic warfare against the Tehran regime and are regarded as significant threats to the nation's cohesion. Other separatist elements include the Turkomans, Afghans, Azerbaijanis and Khuzistanis. In fact, nearly 40 per cent of Iran's population is non-Persian. The regime has vigorously fought these challenges. In 1982, for example, four divisions of the regular army launched an offensive against the Kurds.[79] There is dissatisfaction of a non-ethnic sort as well. The repression of the Baha'is has created a significant source of discontent. Much opposition comes, in addition, from the left which has been weakened, but not destroyed, by the regime. The left includes the Tudeh Party (officially banned by Khomeini in May 1983), the Islamic Mujahedeen with some 10 000 supporters whose leadership (under Masud Rajavi) is now based in Paris, and the Marxist Fedayeen with approximately 8 000 well-organized adherents. The treatment received by the regular army at the hands of the current regime might also qualify it as a possibly disaffected and, by its nature, powerful group.

A number of major sources of opposition thus currently exist within Iran. They simmer just below the surface and may boil over before very long. Two circumstances make the possibility real and maybe imminent. In the first place, the end of the war between Iran and Iraq might weaken the sense of national purpose that it had managed to generate. The removal of this source of cohesion could give full vent to the sectarian, ideological and other frustrations which are embedded in the nation's political fabric. Second, there will be the consquences which follow from the death of Ayatollah Ruhollah Khomeini. His death will deprive the country of the only personality who, through a combination of ruthless repression and religious appeal, is capable of maintaining some degree of unity.

It is simply a matter of relative likelihoods, but let us assume that, of the nations just surveyed, the major instability will be experienced by post-Khomeini Iran. What might the implications be? The geostrategic significance assigned to Iran by the USA is well known, as is the importance which Washington attaches to a pro-US—or at least anti-Soviet—regime. Iran's place in Soviet security calculations is usually less well appreciated in spite of the fact that the USSR has for many decades regarded the Persian Gulf, and Iran in particular, as part of its security perimeter. The area is viewed as a base for foreign intrigues and possible military operations against the USSR. US endeavours to establish security ties to the region in the form of the Baghdad Pact and CENTO, and subsequent efforts to arm the Shah have re-inforced Soviet fears in this regard. A servile, or at least, responsive Iran would thus almost certainly be welcome from Moscow's perspective (particularly since this would buttress the Soviet position *vis-à-vis* China as well as the West). Finally—and one may easily exaggerate on this score—influence over Iranian politics would also provide the Kremlin with some leverage over the West's oil supplies. Thus, for a combination of offensive and defensive reasons, neither superpower could regard massive political instability in Iran with passive equanimity. How would they respond to such a situation?

Stage I: covert responses to extreme instability in Iran

Given the costs and risks of an outright bid at a military take-over, both sides would probably respond to evidence of major turmoil in the country with intensified, and largely covert, attempts to strengthen the position of the Iranian political faction whose policies were most consonant with the super-power's own interests and values; covert activity would also be aimed at undermining the domestic forces whose fortunes were being promoted by the adversary.

For the USSR, the obvious candidate for support would be the Tudeh Party. Though currently banned, the organization's infrastructure has probably survived and the party may well be a force to contend with after the Ayatollah's death. Moscow might hedge its bets by supporting the leftist Mujahedeen and Fedayeen groups as well. For the USA, the choice would probably fall on some portion of the armed services—perhaps the air force—which has, of course, benefited enormously from US weapons and training in the days of the Shah. The hope here would be for a pro-Western—or at least anti-Soviet—military regime depending on the USA for its military equipment and other forms of assistance. Something along the lines of the regimes established by Muhammed Zia ul-Haq in Pakistan or by Kenan Evren in Turkey might be envisaged. The initial stage would thus be characterized by intense, competitive, covert action accompanied by the usual measure of Cold War rhetoric.

De-escalation could occur as early as this if a neutral and stable domestic political force were to emerge, one whose leadership would be more acceptable to both superpowers than the perils of escalating involvement. But it is not at all obvious that such a political force would be waiting in the wings or that it could be created. This scenario should thus be expected to have additional stages.

Stage II: the militarization of the crisis

A transition from covert subversive activities to overt military action would characterize this stage and the sequence of events would largely depend on which side appeared to be winning the covert struggle. If the pro-Soviet faction was scoring major victories, it is quite conceivable that the USA would take more forceful action. The view that Iran might become responsive to Soviet interest coupled with fears that Iran's oil wealth might fall into Soviet hands and worries about the implications for the future of Saudi Arabia and Oman, could cause Washington to opt for direct military intervention.[80] But an attempt to occupy the whole country would tax the practical capacity of even the USCENTCOM and would bring US troops dangerously close to the Soviet border. Besides, most of the desired results would not require a full-scale invasion and occupation. They could, rather, be obtained at a lower cost and with less risk by seizing the province of Khuzestan in the south-west. (Khuzestan is the region where Iran's principal oil installations are located.) This is the assumed US response to imminent Soviet victory in the covert struggle.

What of the position if the covert struggle was being won by the USA (even if it had undertaken no direct military action)? A Soviet attempt to move into Iran with a major invading force—some 26 divisions—designed to occupy the whole country is also improbable. This is not the sort of situation which typically justifies major military risks from Moscow's standpoint—particularly in the face of US warnings and regional military deployments. The logistics of such an operation would, in any event, be exceedingly difficult. Forces at present committed to Afghanistan would have to be included and considerable prior mobilization would also be necessary. Even if the forces were mustered, there would be formidable problems in moving the ground forces—including armour and other heavy equipment—by land over long distances, through difficult terrain and in the face of military resistance from the Iranians and even the USCENTCOM. Invasion forces could take the western route, crossing 3 000 kilometres from the Balkans via Baghdad[81]—a highly implausible undertaking. Another possible route leads from the Caucasus to Kuwait through the Zagro mountain wall. This involves a 1 600-kilometre journey through extremely tortuous terrain subject to interdiction attacks.[82] Pushing southwards, the aggressors would require extensive air cover and would have to use airborne forces in order to seize important transportation and communication nodes. But Soviet airlift capacity is modest (see page 43) and southern Iran is outside the reach of most Soviet fighter/attack aircraft based in the USSR. Air bases in Afghanistan would mitigate the difficulties of air support but would not resolve them. On the whole, the option that best corresponds to Soviet capabilities would be a limited occupation of the north-western part of Iran—Azerbaijan[83] and, possibly, Kurdistan. In this case it would actually be possible to present the USA with a *fait accompli* and from this position Moscow could better exercise pressure on the central government in Iran as well as on neighbouring states.

A partial move into Iran would thus seem to be the likely response of either superpower to an imminent covert victory by its rival. Assuming that one of the two superpowers did choose this path, how would the other superpower respond? It is unlikely that it would seek to evict the occupier by a counter-offensive into the occupied area. The military advantage would obviously lie with the defender and the escalatory risks of joining battle with the rival would be enormous. Rather, it would simply seize the *other* region in a compensatory action—Khuzestan or Azerbaijan and Kurdistan depending on the superpower—and seek to undermine its opponent's interests in the Gulf by less direct military activity.

Let us assume that the USA has taken the initiative by occupying Khuzestan. The Soviet Union then moves into north-western Iran which, nevertheless, puts them at something of a disadvantage. What might the USSR do next? It could seek to jeopardize US interests through local proxies. For example, Iraq might be incited to move against Kuwait, or South Yemen could perhaps seek to rekindle the Dhofar rebellion in Oman. Success in such a venture could partially compensate for the US presence in Khuzestan and US military assistance to a beleaguered friend could further strain its military resources in the region.

At a somewhat higher level of escalation, the USSR could decide to attack US oil shipping directly. It might, for instance, mine Hormuz or sink a few ships in the straits in order to impede passage to and from the Gulf. It could even launch submarine attacks on US tankers. Even a few sinkings could cause tanker commerce to dwindle due to increased insurance rates for ships in this area and because of the unwillingness of civilian crews to undertake the voyage. Thus, with modest human loss, Western oil supplies could be seriously endangered. Whether such attacks would actually occur is open to question. The Soviet Union is also heavily dependent on Indian Ocean SLOCs (for commerce between European and Asian USSR)[84] and these could easily be the object of retaliatory disruption.[85] Nevertheless this possibility cannot be entirely dismissed.

If operations of this kind did take place in the Persian Gulf, how might they affect the security of European nations? Several possibilities suggest themselves. To begin with, US troops and equipment in transit to the Gulf area would require some *en route* assistance involving facilities in Portugal, Spain and possibly other members of the Atlantic Alliance as well. Several NATO countries would thus become indirect participants in the military activity and, at the very least, East–West relations within Europe would have been damaged. However, direct military retaliation against these NATO countries would not be the Soviet Union's most likely course of action. Such action is potentially a cause of very serious escalation and probably ineffective as well. (It would, for example, be very hard to destroy West European airfields with conventional weapons and with long-distance sorties over hostile airspace.)

The USSR could, however, engage in some *horizontal* escalation of its own by putting military pressure on US allies and interests elsewhere in the world. For example, it could stir up trouble for South Korea. The Kremlin could also deflect US attention and resources from the Persian Gulf by engineering a crisis over West Berlin which would fall short of an invasion—for example, by blocking access routes to the city. At the very least, the effect would be to unsettle Washington's priorities and to induce Western Europe to seek a re-allocation of US forces to Europe and away from the Gulf.

Even at this point, the crisis could be managed without further escalation, although this would call for a major exertion of political will. To begin with, a mutually acceptable political solution for Iran would be required. Such a solution could take several forms. A starting point might be a divided state—along Korean lines—with eventual reunification under internationally guaranteed neutrality. On that basis, measures could perhaps be taken to demilitarize the area. Most such solutions would, however, be less than optimal from the point of view of both superpowers and efforts to resolve the conflict at this stage might be unsuccessful.

Stage III: further escalation and expanded European involvement

Of all the NATO nations, Turkey would be most rapidly exposed to the risk of direct military involvement. There are numerous ways in which it could be drawn into the conflict. Three of these stand out as being particularly likely.

1. If the Soviet Union were to undertake significant airlift operations towards the Gulf area these could require flying over Turkey, thus causing the possibility of aerial combat over Turkish territory.

2. Given the importance of the Turkish-based communications facilities for US operations in the region, these installations could be the object of pre-emptive or retaliatory Soviet action. Soviet aircraft or missiles could, for example, attack the long-range radar and communications complex at Pirinclik near Diyarbakir or various NADGE stations. Strikes could also be launched against pre-positioned ammunition sites, petroleum, oil and lubricants (POL) depots and so forth. While the collateral damage of such operations might not be very extensive, there would be considerable potential for escalating military activity in Turkey.

3. The USA might use military bases in Turkey for the intermediate basing of some portion of its airlifted troops (for example, some parts of the 82nd

Airborne Division). Such a move could be designed to bring the troops up to the theatre—thus intimidating the USSR—without actually committing them to combat—thus avoiding further escalation. But Moscow might not view things quite in this way and the consequences for Turkey could be significant. Anticipating the imminent combat deployment of these troops very close to Soviet territory, the USSR might seek to pre-empt by attacking the basing facilities. Such action would, of course, carry escalatory risks, but in this region the Kremlin might rely on its SS-20 missiles and Backfire bombers—possibly also SS-22 missiles—for escalation control. Specifically it might reason that this theatre nuclear capacity should deter a US response by demonstrating that the Soviet Union could escalate to a slightly higher level of destruction while staying short of the strategic threshold.

In each of these three cases Turkey's allies could be called upon for assistance. At a low level of involvement, for example, European merchant shipping could be enlisted to assist Persian Gulf deployment. More significantly, a Soviet attack on Turkish territory would trigger the military mechanisms of collective security and a NATO response could take various forms. Finally, other West European countries could be drawn into the military engagement even beyond their alliance commitments. Were Oman to become involved—by naval operations for the control of Hormuz or, say, by action to deter armed pressure from South Yemen—for example, the UK might also become embroiled to some extent. There are some 100 seconded British military personnel in Oman as well as approximately 240 military men on contract.[86] The confrontation could also spread in other ways.

Stage IV: expansion of the conflict to the Horn of Africa and the possibility of French involvement

At this stage, or even earlier, the conflict could assume the form of naval warfare. This might take place because of an explicit bilateral intent. It has been suggested, for example, that the desire to save oil installations from destruction could cause both superpowers to limit most of their military operations to thrusts and parries at sea.[87] But naval restraint may be difficult to reconcile with military practice and doctrine, or with the political pressures that each superpower would probably experience at such a time.

The security of SLOCs would, in any event, be a major concern on both sides and a crucial priority would be to secure control of the Bab-al-Mandaab Strait. The USSR might use its military facilities in Ethiopia and South Yemen—each nation being on opposite sides of the waterway—to deny Western passage between the Red Sea and the Indian Ocean. If it did so, or if the USA assumed that it would do so, attacks against these installations should be expected. The fact that submarine facilities seem to have been developed on the Dahlak Islands and in Aden—from which SSNs or cruise-missile carrying submarines could operate—makes these bases obvious military targets. The same appplies to airfields at Asmara (near Dahlak) and in Aden. There is, moreover, no reason to suppose that Soviet airfields in Afghanistan—from which Backfire bombers could cover the waters around the Horn of Africa—would be spared. US installations would also be open to Soviet attack—for example, the US airfield at Masirah off the coast of Oman.

At this point, military activity would have assumed a more direct form. No longer would it be a matter of undermining the rival superpower's interests in other parts of the world or of actions undertaken by Persian Gulf proxies. Escalation could continue on its upward path and two, mutually compatible possibilities should be considered. The Soviet Union might, for example, use nuclear-armed Backfire bombers against carrier battle groups in the north-west quadrant of the Indian Ocean. Or a US attack on Aden might provoke retaliation with SS-20s against, say, Saudi Arabia. The USA itself could use SLCMs with ground-attack capabilities (that is, the TLAM-N carrying a 200-kt warhead with a range of 2 700 kilometres) as an exercise in controlled escalation. The threshold between conventional and nuclear warfare could thus be crossed in various ways and a major psychological barrier to all-out escalation removed in this way, initial intentions notwithstanding.

The confrontation could escalate horizontally in yet another way. By bringing the conflict to the Horn of Africa, and consequently to the Cape route, the issue of the role of French forces would be raised. The extent of France's force-projection capacity has been described. Though this is by no means inevitable, France could be drawn into the conflict through a combination of perceived national interest and US pressure. Military activity involving France might be limited to action designed to secure the Mozambique Channel and French minesweepers at Djibouti could be called upon to clear the Bab-al-Mandaab Strait if it were mined by the Soviet Union. The French role could also, though less plausibly, extend to participation in operations against Soviet bases in Ethiopia and South Yemen.

The overall level of tension and combat at this stage would be a threat to crisis stability within Europe itself.[88] De-escalation might still be feasible but less so than at earlier stages.

Stage V: horizontal escalation and the northern flank

If Soviet activities in the Persian Gulf and the Horn of Africa were to place the USA at a major military disadvantage and jeopardize interests which it deems fundamental, a counter-offensive in the northern seas would, as suggested in chapter 3, be a real possibility. This could occur in several ways and at various levels of escalatory intensity. First, the USA, along with other NATO partners, could engage in forward SSN operations. Such a course could be pursued if the strategy of interdicting Soviet attack submarines at the GIUK and Bear Island Gaps was not considered sufficiently effective. Offensive action against the Soviet Northern Fleet might then be considered necessary and while such action could be limited to warfare against SSNs, it could also extend to strategic ASW.[89] In the latter case the Soviet Union might be tempted to launch their SLBMs in a 'use them or lose them' context, in which case an all-out nuclear confrontation would be initiated.

Second, battle group assaults could be launched against the Northern Fleet and its bases on the Kola Peninsula. Again, the idea would be both to destroy Soviet attack submarines, before they could interfere with Atlantic SLOCs, and SSBNs before they could undertake strategic missions. There is yet a third possibility that does not assume actual offensive action by the USA: the Soviet Union could decide to launch a pre-emptive attack against military facilities in northern Norway. Given the possible function of Norwegian bases for strikes against the Kola Peninsula, and given the importance of intelligence-gathering facilities in the north of Norway, point attacks by Soviet forces against these installations would be entirely conceivable. A NATO counter-offensive would be the logical sequel.

In each of these cases, substantial NATO involvement would be virtually inevitable. In each case, the pressures for vertical escalation would be substantial. At this stage both the northern flank (through Norway) and the southern flank (via Turkey) would be directly involved in the confrontation. Even if France and Great Britain managed to avoid involvement in Stage IV, and even if the use of LRTNFs did not yet extend beyond the Persian Gulf and the Horn of Africa, the military engagement of these two flanks would make a spread of hostilities to the central front more likely. The attendant air battles, massive movements of ground forces and possible use of nuclear options would remove any ceiling to the level of destruction which might afflict Europe. While it has been assumed that the conflict was sparked in Iran, other crises originating in the Persian Gulf could lead to roughly similar consequences.

III. An Arab–Israeli conflict

Most people would probably regard an Arab–Israeli conflict as the most likely source of an ultimately global confrontation. The seemingly insoluble conflicts of interest and insurmountable hatreds in the Middle East, the intensive militarization of the countries involved and the role which these countries play in the superpowers' calculations and commitments, explain why this should be so. An Arab–Israeli conflict could have distinctive escalatory consequences and most importantly, such a conflict could spread much more rapidly and carry greater risks of vertical escalation than the previous scenario, since it would be driven more by immediate military imperatives than by pondered political decisions.

Because of the risk of rapid vertical escalation, both sides, partly prompted by an awareness of the risks, have so far exerted themselves to avoid a confrontation in this part of the world. There were major crises in 1967, 1973 and 1982 but these were reasonably well managed by both superpowers.[90] However, the experiences of the past may not apply to possible future crises, since the context in which future crises might occur has changed in several important ways.

To begin with, each side has demonstrated a growing willingness to establish a direct military presence in the region and this might impair the ability of the superpowers to remain detached from future conflicts. A major contingent of US marines participated in the multinational force in Beirut. Marines were originally stationed offshore so that "all necessary" measures could be taken to "assure the safety" of the troops already on shore.[91] US naval forces participated actively in military operations against Lebanese Muslin and Syrian positions in Lebanon (see page 85). The USA has not engaged in such direct and extensive military involvement in the region since 1958. The USA has, in addition, an 800-strong detachment from the 101st Air-Assault Division participating in the multinational force observing compliance with the Egyptian–Israeli peace agreements.

The USSR has also insinuated itself into the area. At the time of writing there are some 8 000 Soviet military advisers in Syria, including the 500–600 Soviet crewmen manning each of the two SAM-5 missile sites that were established in 1983. The readiness of both sides to dispatch forces to the area means that future crises may be stoked with more volatile kindling than ever before.

Second, it is apparent that the naval deployments of both sides are guided by doctrines in which offensive operations occupy an ever more accepted place. And this, moreover, at a time when nuclear-tipped short-range weapons and cruise missiles form a growing part of the arsenals carried by superpower armadas (see page 23).

Finally, relations between the two superpowers are now considerably more strained than they were at the time of the principal crises of the past. Hence, if the regional situation should take a dramatic turn for the worse, effective communication and constructive compromise may be more difficult to arrange than, say, in 1973. Thus, in yet another respect, past successes at crisis management may not be repeated in the future. Such is the background for the scenario. Elements of it may change in due course but major modifications should not be expected in the near future.

Stage I: major fighting erupts in the Middle East

A new Arab–Israeli conflict could be ignited in several ways and the probability of each of these ways will necessarily change with time. A major confrontation could be precipitated by an Israeli decision to annex the West Bank and Gaza, or by a Syrian move—buttressed by the Soviet presence—to retake the occupied Golan Heights. The escalatory consequences of various types of initial crisis may be similar but, at present, the obvious flashpoint is

Lebanon. There the conflicting interests of the several domestic and foreign protagonists seem virtually irreconcilable in anything but the very long run and external military interventions are unlikely to alter this fact.

A superpower collision in this region could, in principle, be caused in at least two distinct ways. To begin with, a renewed US entanglement in Lebanon could produce a clash in a very direct fashion. For example, US operations against Syrian positions in that country—assaulting Moscow's principal client in the region and threatening the USSR's own military installations—could spark a conflict between the superpowers. One should not, however, overstate the risks of marching towards war along a straight path. The more directly obvious the danger, the stronger is the impulse towards prudence; that is, dangerous acts can most readily be avoided when their consequences are clearly apparent. This is particularly the case when, from the outset, decisions are guided by political rather than purely military logic. Thus it may be that the greatest peril lies in a situation over which the two nations have less immediate control, one which, for example, is dominated by the activities of their principal regional allies. The danger would be particularly acute if, by the nature of the crisis, considerations of a military sort were to override those of a more political character.

Let us assume in a situation of this kind, one that would, in all likelihood, originate with an Israeli–Syrian confrontation. Let us assume, furthermore, that the USA showed no interest in having its troops in the area participate in what would now have become an international conflict rather than a civil war. How might the superpowers, nevertheless, be drawn into a military collision and what pressures for horizontal and vertical escalation might develop?

Stage II: superpower involvement and the naval tinderbox

As fighting erupts between Israel and Syria (and possibly other Arab states as well), the presence of the two Soviet SAM-5 batteries would be of major military concern to the Israeli side. These surface-to-air missiles were introduced after the rout of Syria and the PLO in 1982. Their military purpose was to bolster Syria's air defences which, in the course of the invasion of Lebanon, had proved totally inadequate against Israel's air power. An associated Soviet intent was to regain some of the prestige and leverage lost after the defeats suffered by its protégés using Soviet military equipment. The two SAM-5 installations, each manned by over 500 Soviet soldiers, were set up in the Syrian towns of Dumeir (30 kilometres north-east of Damascus) and Homs (near Lebanon's north-eastern border). With a 240-kilometre range, the missiles would represent a substantial threat to Israel's command and control aircraft as well as to its warplanes. In the heat of the fighting, and as military imperatives come to dominate other considerations, the Israelis could decide to strike at the SAM-5s despite the presence of large Soviet crews. They might count on the Kremlin exercising the self-restraint that it has practised during previous incidents, but such an expectation could be ill-founded. Some damage has been inflicted on Soviet property during past Middle East conflicts[92] but, in this case, the magnitude of the assault and the number of Soviet lives lost would have no precedent. The Soviet Union's battered international image, its influence in the Arab world and its status as a decisive superpower to be reckoned with would receive a major—Moscow might fear terminal—blow in the absence of a forceful response. Consequently, militarily meaningful action would probably be contemplated.

The USSR might consider an air attack on Israeli positions in the Lebanon or even on targets within Israel itself. Although such action would no doubt be accompanied by assurances to Washington of the limited aims of the Soviet retaliation, the escalatory perils would be apparent and the Kremlin has typically avoided overly provocative behaviour. Moreover, there would be immediate military risks. (It would be extremely embarrassing to have Soviet aircraft brought down by the Israelis.) For these reasons, a response short of an actual military attack would seem more likely. A major show of naval force could be the chosen course. The Soviet Navy did undertake some manoeuvres during the crises of 1967 and 1973 but these were, for the most part, symbolic and non-offensive in nature. Such limited activity might simply not suffice under the assumed circumstances. Instead, substantial naval forces could be deployed off Beirut and Israel, mock runs towards shore could be staged, amphibious exercises could be conducted and so forth. Such a course of action might be perceived as demonstrating firmness and yet would fall short of outright warfare against Israel. Assuming that it would be chosen, how would the USA react?

The US response would probably be guided, at least initially, by a notion of controlled reciprocity. US domestic politics would permit no less. The obvious first move would be to augment the US naval presence in the region up to or even beyond the level in autumn 1983. In addition, US surface combatants would engage in naval manoeuvres some of which might also have a pronounced offensive character. US ships could also interpose themselves between Soviet vessels and the Israeli coastline where possible. A world-wide alert of US forces, as in October 1973, might also be called.

The confrontation might, of course, go no further than this. Both sides have some experience of managing naval crises,[93] the Hot Line would no doubt be extensively used and the disentangling of the superpowers' navies could, in principle, be arranged at this stage. De-escalation could also be promoted if both sides were to rein in their Syrian and Israeli allies,[94] always assuming that this was possible. Things could, nevertheless, go wrong and the crisis could rapidly get out of control. Both sides maintain a substantial naval presence in the area. The Sixth Fleet, which when assigned to NATO becomes STRIK-FORSOUTH (Naval Striking and Support Force Southern Europe), is usually composed of more than 40 ships and 200 aircraft. The fleet includes, *inter alia*, two attack-carrier striking forces and an amphibious task force.[95] The USSR maintains a more modest presence in the form of the Soviet Mediterranean Squadron (or Fifth Eskadra). While the size of the Soviet squadron fluctuates, it typically includes 8–10 submarines and 30–40 surface ships, of which, however, 15–20 are auxiliary ships.[96] This force is drawn principally from the Soviet Black Sea Fleet and, for submarines in particular, from its Northern Fleet.

Crisis instability would result from assumptions held by each side about the other's probable naval behaviour. The Soviet scenario for a conflict in the eastern Mediterranean, as revealed in deployments and manoeuvres during previous crises, is to act very rapidly to inflict maximum damage on US carrier groups. This strategy is based on two concerns. The first concern is that the US Sixth Fleet's naval aircraft are theoretically capable of launching attacks against the south-western USSR from positions in the eastern Mediterranean. This particular capability will be enhanced by the deployment of SLCMs. The Soviet Union would thus wish to strike immediately before a tactical—and hence conceivable—nuclear attack could be directed at its own territory. The second concern is that the Sixth Fleet's superiority implies that most of the Soviet ships would be destroyed before long. Consequently, a maximum amount of *pre-emptive* damage would be called for from the Soviet standpoint. Towards this end, and as tensions mounted, Soviet surface ships and submarines would be pre-positioned within range of US carrier groups, as they were after the US alert in 1973. At the moment that hostilities broke out, or seemed inevitable and imminent, intensive missile strikes[97] would probably be launched against the carriers (which account for most of the US firepower and airpower in the region). United States command authorities are obviously aware of this likelihood and would be loath to allow the Soviet Union a massive first blow. Accordingly, both sides have a strong incentive to pre-empt the other and this, of course, makes for a very unstable and trigger-happy situation.

Although the crisis might be brought under control before a naval conflict erupted, this is by no means certain. There are many ways in which crisis management could fail. An accidental firing could occur. A breakdown in command and control is possible. Intense distrust could vitiate effective diplomacy and so forth. None of these contingencies is outlandish. They may not be particularly probable but they are not altogether impossible. Let us assume, therefore, that crisis management does indeed collapse and that a naval conflict erupts between the USA and the USSR. Such a conflict would probably involve an all-out naval shoot-out between US and Soviet naval vessels. From this point on, de-escalation would become improbable. It must be assumed that events would unfold very rapidly and while military developments would initially be shaped by naval dynamics, conflict could escalate in various ways, both vertically and horizontally, and a number of European nations would be quickly drawn into the engagement. The anticipated speed of the development of the conflagration makes it, perhaps, more natural to think in terms of sub-stages of a single major stage rather than in terms of a sequence of several distinct stages.

Stage IIIA : rapid escalation and the involvement of Balkan nations

Because of its geostrategic location, Turkey might well be the first European victim of the flare-up. An immediate military imperative for the Soviet Union would be to send naval reinforcements from the Black Sea to the eastern Mediterranean. This, in turn, would require passage through the Bosphorus and the Dardanelles which the Western side would seek to block at the very outset. A major responsibility in this regard would almost certainly devolve upon Turkey[98] which could thus become directly dragged into a naval conflict with unpredictable consequences. But this would not be all. In order to secure the Turkish Straits, the Soviet Union might attempt to seize Turkish Thrace. (This is Turkey's only foothold in Europe and one of its most densely populated and developed areas.) With this aim, the USSR might launch an assault at the very beginning of the conflict involving large, mobile ground forces combined with airborne troops and small amphibious landings in the enemy's rear. Thus Turkey's lot might consist of both a land war and Soviet occupation of Thrace.

Although the Kremlin might emphasize the US–Soviet aspect of the conflict and play down its European dimension, declamations to this effect would have a hollow ring. A member of NATO would have been the victim of direct aggression and from this instant on, the two blocs could be pitted against each other. This would provide ample scope for horizontal escalation and there are many ways in which such a conflict could spread even to the central front. Nonetheless, for the moment we shall concentrate on the Mediterranean region and on the naval conflict which we assume to be intense.

In the first place, and in order to facilitate the operation of its surface combatants, the USSR might—again at the very outset—try to seize bases and harbours in northern Greece. While this could be attempted with amphibious action combined with extensive air cover, the USSR might, as in the case of Turkish Thrace, decide on an invasion by land. In either case, direct combat on Greek territory would follow. It is, moreover, likely that Greece would be implicated in the naval conflict as well. It should be understood that even if the Turkish Straits did fall into the Kremlin's hands, Soviet naval forces would still have difficulty penetrating into the Mediterranean as long as NATO retained control of the Aegean. To maintain NATO control of the Aegean, the Greek Navy would be called upon to undertake mine-laying operations and submarine warfare against Soviet vessels in the Aegean and Crete Straits.[99] The case of Greece would thus, in many respects, resemble that of Turkey as both became caught up in the expanding superpower conflict.

The expansion of the conflict would not necessarily discriminate against WTO countries. For example, the Soviet surge towards Thrace over land would necessarily require transit through Bulgaria and might even involve Bulgarian armed forces while NATO's attempts to ward off the invasion could not be expected to spare Bulgarian territory. At all times, both sides would experience considerable pressure to pursue operations with tactical nuclear weapons.

Stage IIIB: the westward spread of the conflict

Turkey and Greece, because of their geographical proximity to the theatre of conflict, would be the earliest European victims. But the spread of the conflict would not be limited to nations in the immediate vicinity of the initial clash. In all likelihood, other European countries in the Mediterranean region would rapidly become involved.

The Sicilian-based GLCMs at Comiso are well suited for military missions in an eastern Mediterranean/Middle Eastern theatre and could be called upon to perform a variety of functions if fighting spread to the Balkans. Their use would almost inevitably produce some form of Soviet retaliation against Italy or other members of the Atlantic Alliance. Even if a GLCM launch merely appeared imminent, a pre-emptive strike against Comiso would probably be undertaken. This could take the form of bomber raids, possibly with aircraft based in Libya,[100] or it could even involve the use of SS-20s—for which Sicily would be within easy reach. Here again, a direct strike against a NATO member would tend to redefine the confrontation as one between blocs rather than merely bloc leaders.

Even if LRTNFs were not used, non-Balkan European countries could become involved in the conflict in various other ways. The need, from a Western point of view, has been stressed of bottling up the Soviet Navy in the Black Sea by closing the Dardanelles and the Bosphorus. Similar reasoning would apply to other entrances into the Mediterranean since the Soviet Union could dispatch naval reinforcements from the Northern and Baltic fleets as well. However, given the distances involved, the naval battle in the eastern Mediterranean would probably have been concluded to the Sixth Fleet's advantage by the time that reinforcements arrived and it would thus not be sensible to send many additional surface combatants to the area. Attack submarines could, nevertheless, play an important role for the USSR even at this stage. They could continue to threaten enemy naval vessels, making it harder for the West to support its southern flank operations with sea-based aircraft and firepower as well as with amphibious troops. NATO's Mediterranean SLOCs could also be disrupted, providing Moscow with additional means of pressure against the USA and its allies. Finally, SSBNs deployed in the area by the USA would present a continuous danger to the USSR—particularly since the TLAM-Ns would have the entire Ukraine and parts of Russia within their range. As a consequence, Soviet submarines might be required to attack these SSBNs. Most of the reinforcements would probably come from the Northern Fleet (from which additional Soviet submarines were dispatched at the time of the US alert of October 1973) and, to a somewhat lesser extent, from the Baltic Fleet.

In these circumstances, a major effort would be made to close Gibraltar to

Soviet submarines seeking entry into the Mediterranean. Such an effort would involve naval operations by Spain, Portugal and probably the United Kingdom as well as the USA.[101] As a result, the conflict would have spread not only to the western Mediterranean but to the Atlantic as well. France, which is both a Mediterranean and an Atlantic country, could soon be called upon for logistic and combat assistance which, if the fighting had indeed spread in the suggested direction, it would probably be willing to provide.[102]

Stage IIIC: expansion to the northern flank

The position of the northern flank might be similar to that which it was assumed to have in the Persian Gulf scenario. That is, if the USSR was doing reasonably well in the Mediterranean, or had taken the initiative in escalating the level of conflict, the USA might decide to launch a compensatory counter-offensive in the northern seas. Efforts would surely be made to interdict Soviet submarines from the northern seas as they sought to move towards the Mediterranean. This would require two sorts of operations. To begin with, the Danish Straits would be sealed in order to block Soviet vessels in the Baltic Sea. As a result of this, Denmark would be caught up in the confrontation and Soviet action against this member of NATO could be expected. In addition, every attempt would be made to impose as high a rate of attrition as possible on enemy submarines as they passed through the GIUK and Bear Island Gaps. Again, and as part of the campaign, the USA might launch offensive operations against the Kola Peninsula and this would mean that Norwegian troops, though not necessarily ground forces, would be drawn into direct combat with Soviet forces. Norway could, of course, fall victim to a pre-emptive Soviet invasion (followed, in all likelihood, by a NATO counter-offensive).

At this point the war would have spread to much of Europe, but this geographical spread is only one aspect of the potential escalation. It is impossible to separate the risks of horizontal and vertical escalation in this scenario or to think of the two sorts of danger as appearing in a distinct chronological order. Pressures for vertical escalation would, indeed, be experienced from the very beginning and at virtually every instant thereafter. The need to inflict massive pre-emptive blows, the density of nuclear weapons in these regions and the offensive bent of current Soviet and US military doctrines militate against the limitation to combat of conventional weapons.

Much of the danger of crossing the nuclear threshold would appear as early as the initial naval encounter. The idea of using tactical nuclear weapons for conflicts at sea has gained considerable respectability in the US naval literature.[103] As one prize-winning naval essayist recently pointed out: "We must begin training in offensive nuclear warfare as well as in defensive measures.... We must include the requirements for victory in tactical nuclear warfare in our force structure planning".[104] Similar thoughts have probably been running through Soviet minds. Soviet doctrine has always stressed deterrence by denial rather than by assured punishment and has thus emphasized war-fighting in both conventional and nuclear settings. Moreover, if the USSR's perceived imperative in a Mediterranean naval battle is the rapid destruction of US carrier forces, then tactical nuclear weapons are the most effective means of bringing this about. In discussing possible US–Soviet naval confrontation, a study published by the US Congressional Budget Office in 1982 pointed out that "the temptation [to use nuclear weapons] would be great, given the difficulty of defeating a battle group with conventional weapons".[105] Even if a carrier were outside the radius within which the ship itself would be directly destroyed by a nuclear blast, the blast could still damage shipboard weapons and derange antennas and other exposed instruments. At the same time the EMP (electro-magnetic pulse) produced by the detonation would impair the vessel's electronic equipment. The deployment in 1980 of a new Soviet anti-ship cruise missile with a nuclear warhead (the SS-N-19) is consistent with a nuclear naval strategy.

Either side might calculate that the limited collateral damage caused by the use of nuclear weapons at sea would dampen escalatory impulses. But a psychological obstacle to nuclear warfare at any level would have been removed and the use of tactical or theatre nuclear weapons—and perhaps escalation to the strategic level—would have been made more likely as a result. In any case, as the outspoken US Secretary of the Navy John Lehman recently admitted: "should deterrence break down between the navies of the United States and the Soviet Union, it will be instantaneously a global naval conflict".[106]

Nuclear weapons could be used at the very beginning in a non-naval setting as well. For example, a nuclear-arms storage site is believed to be located at Erzurum, Turkey (less than 300 kilometres from the Soviet border). If Turkey fell victim to a Soviet invasion—in either this or the Persian Gulf scenario—and if it seemed likely that Erzurum might be overrun, these weapons could be used with the 'use them or lose them' rationale. As such sites seem also to exist in Greece, a similar reasoning would apply to that country as well.

No matter what the nature of the original battles, as the conflict spread westwards and as pressures for its expansion to the central front developed, the probability that either tactical or theatre nuclear weapons would be used must be expected to increase substantially. In this scenario, as distinct from the case in which the conflict originates in the Persian Gulf, the escalatory process would run its course very rapidly. While it might take several months for the previous scenario to play itself out, in the present case a period of no more than a few weeks, perhaps less, seems more likely.

IV. Conclusions

If these scenarios are accepted as being generally credible, what conclusions are we to draw from them? Specific policy recommendations will be discussed in the following chapter but several broad impressions are obvious at this point. In the first place, there is no need to assume an explicit decision, either before the crisis or at the outbreak of the regional conflict, on the part of either superpower to engage in direct military action against the other superpower. Yet such military action might well occur for various reasons, including the pressure of perceived military needs, a breakdown in the diplomatic requisites for crisis management or the inability of decision-makers to trace the consequences of current decisions down a sufficiently long causal path. There is nothing new about this sort of thing and history is full of examples of major conflicts erupting in spite of their protagonists never having intended them to. Historical lessons are seldom learned, however, and this time the consequences may be far more serious than before.

Second, European involvements in the military confrontations initiated or fuelled by the superpowers would not spring from clearly defined decisions based on careful assessment of the costs and benefits of defending the bloc leaders' Third World interests. It is, in fact, ridiculous to suppose that the European stakes in, say, the political future of Iran or the outcome of the Arab–Israeli conflict would even remotely justify the consequences that these scenarios imply.

For those European nations most distant from the initial engagement, the conflict would probably come to their doorstep through a sequence of events that had been unforeseen and over which—with some exceptions—they have but minimal control. For those countries physically closest to the initial confrontation, their geographical location and assigned military roles would implicate them virtually at the outset. In neither case would there be any limit to the amount of human and material loss that these nations might suffer.

Appendix. Conflict expansion and probability analysis: an illustrative example

A hypothetical narrative has been provided of how events could unfold in those parts of the Third World where regional conflict most threatens to draw in European nations. The purpose of the exercise was to pin-point the forces which are likely to drive horizontal and vertical escalation and to identify the forms which such escalation might assume. The words 'likely' and 'probable' were used freely in the text in a manner consistent with general usage. However, the reader may wish to consider these matters in more concrete terms by ascribing specific numbers to these notions, that is, to speak of specific numerical probabilities of compound events and to follow these numbers to their precise conclusions.

There is something comforting about assigning numbers to ideas of probability and there may be some benefit in so doing, provided that the exercise is kept in proper perspective. Probabilities are usually assigned to events on the basis of the frequency of occurrence of the event relative to the set of all possibilities (the sample space). For events which have not yet occurred, notions of frequency are obviously inapplicable and the concept of probability is dealt with differently. Knowing that the probability of occurrence of any event can vary between zero and one (i.e., a probability of 0.5 means that there is a 50 per cent, or even, chance of that event happening), we must assign numbers in this range subjectively. For a chain of possible events we then directly estimate overall probabilities from these numbers.

The danger of misplaced specificity would arise if the subjective estimates were mistaken for objective, empirically given realities. It may, nevertheless, be useful to clarify assumptions about likelihood that would otherwise remain implicit—and thus beyond the reach of direct challenge—by assigning explicit probabilities to events. More generally, this procedure allows us to compute probabilities associated with a stochastic process, that is, a sequence of events containing several possibilities at each stage and where, in each case, the outcome depends on some chance element. Our scenarios represent processes of just this sort. Specific *implications* of various assumptions can thus be drawn. These may prove somewhat unexpected. As is the case for scenarios in general, some heuristic benefits may accrue.

We may proceed as follows. In the first instance the set of possible situations should be identified for the various stages of the scenario. A subjective probability is assigned to each possibility. A 'probability tree' can thus be constructed, with the understanding that the numbers pinned to the branches from a particular branching point must add up to one. A 'probability measure' (also called a 'tree measure') can then be defined on the various paths that events could take. The Middle East scenario will be used here for purposes of illustration.

It will be assumed that one of the two crises described above has occurred. This provides a starting point and at this stage—by the terms of our scenario—the major question concerns the probability that a naval conflict between the two superpowers in the eastern Mediterranean will occur. Let us assume that this is not highly likely but nevertheless possible and assign a probability of a naval shoot-out $P_{ns} = 0.2$. (The probability of this not happening is, by implication, $P_{nns} = 1 - P_{ns} = 0.8$.)

At this stage our scenario suggested five alternative situations (S_i), which we list:

S_1 = Crisis stops at level of naval encounter with no further escalation. For the reasons described above, this contingency is theoretically possible but somewhat implausible in practice. Let us assume that $P_{S_1} = 0.1$.

S_2 = Balkan nations become implicated in the conflict with no further horizontal spread. This too is possible but not probable (since the forces that caused the Balkan countries to become involved would, in all likelihood, draw in the western Mediterranean nations, and maybe others, as well). Let us once again assign $P_{S_2} = 0.1$.

S_3 = The Balkan nations *and* those near Gibraltar become embroiled in the US–Soviet conflict but horizontal escalation proceeds no further. This is not entirely implausible; hence assume $P_{S_3} = 0.4$.

S_4 = The conflict involves the northern flank as well. This is certainly possible but let us err on the side of optimism and assume that it is more likely that escalation would stop in the western Mediterranean. $P_{S_4} = 0.3$.

S_5 = A further possibility identified in the scenario would have Italian-based cruise missiles employed in a conflict based in the Balkans and the eastern Mediterranean (but implying no further spread at *this* stage). This outcome is not particularly likely but is conceivable. We will assume $P_{S_5} = 0.1$.

From this stage—played around the initial naval conflict—one might inquire into the possibility of the conflict spreading to central Europe. In each of the situations S_2–S_5, the possibility would be very real but it becomes increasingly likely as the extent of horizontal escalation during the previous stage increases. For each situation S_2–S_5, some probability can be assigned for the conflict spreading to central Europe (ce) or for it not doing so (nce). These probabilities are designated P_{ce} and P_{nce}.

On this basis we have defined a finite stochastic process. It can be described graphically by the following probability tree where for each branch, P_{ce} is assumed to depend on P_{S_i} and subjective probabilities are assigned accordingly.

Figure 8. Probability tree for the eastern Mediterranean scenario

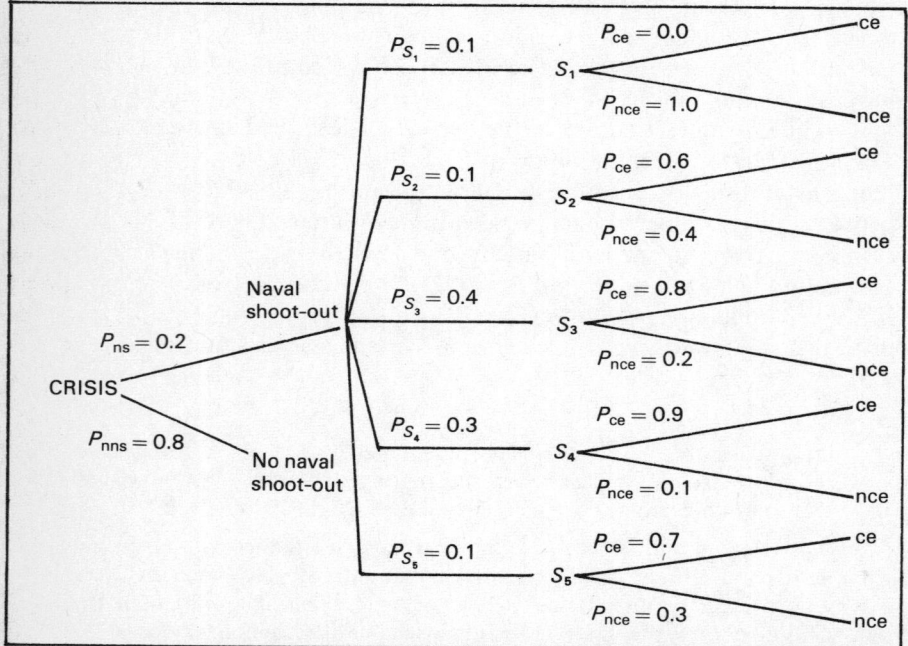

Figure 9. Naval shoot-out and the probability of conflict spreading to central Europe

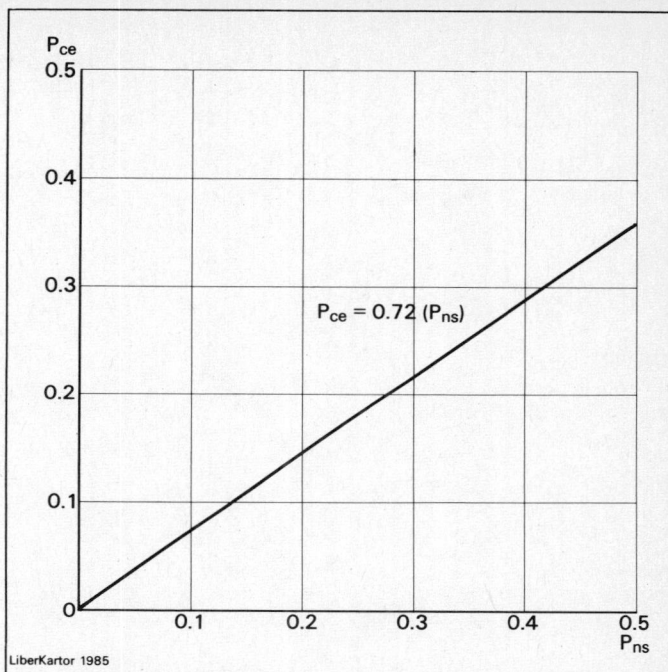

LiberKartor 1985

We now have a basis for calculating the probabilities associated with entire branches of the scenario. For example, we may wish to know the aggregate probability that central Europe would become a participant in warfare by any one of the four paths S_2–S_5. By summing the overall probabilities we obtain a compound probability that a crisis in the Middle East of the type described would lead to such involvement in a superpower war of 0.14. (Whether or not this probability is considered high is a subjective matter.) If, however, we also assume that a naval shoot-out has occurred as a result of the crisis, the probability (across the four paths) of central European entanglement climbs to 0.72—a high figure by any standard.

We can, furthermore, vary our assumptions and examine the consequences of assigning different probabilities to the occurrence of a naval shoot-out (say on a range 0.1–0.5). Graphically this produces the results displayed in figure 9. Clearly, the probability of warfare in central Europe depends very much on how likely we think the naval battle to be. It is of the following algebraic form:

$$P_{ce} = 0.72 P_{ns}$$

which means, for example, that if the probability of a naval shoot-out is 0.5, then the probability of a war in central Europe is 0.36.

The purpose of this exercise is simply to point out that concrete probabilistic assumptions can yield interesting conclusions. We have proceeded in a very simple fashion. Assumptions about horizontal escalation, for example, were made in the absence of assumptions about vertical escalation. More advanced probability analysis—using Markov chains or Bayesian models —could produce rather more sophisticated results.

Chapter 5.   On reducing the risks

I. Introduction

The likely burdens that competing US–Soviet interests in the Third World could place on the security of European nations have now been surveyed. The task of this chapter is to propose ways of managing or mitigating these burdens.

Existing political and military relationships give the USA a substantial ability to implicate other alliance members in its external confrontations. Not only can the USA apply significant leverage to this end but, in addition, the logistics of certain confrontations would make it difficult—though not impossible—for the allies to choose a role for themselves other than that assigned by geopolitical considerations, by the structure of the Alliance, and by the dynamics of conflict escalation. An obvious asymmetry is inherent in such relationships but this asymmetry has, for the most part, been willingly accepted by the nations of Western Europe as the price of their own security.

All NATO members share to *some* extent Washington's concern about Soviet military power and external intentions. They have traditionally welcomed the disproportionate US contribution to the common defence and have, in consequence found it difficult to argue persuasively against the USA's dominant position within the Alliance. This is still a reasonably accurate description of the state of Western affairs though pressures have been mounting for a reassessment of Atlantic relations and what has been true so far may no longer be so in the future.

To begin with, the gap in perceptions concerning the extent of the Soviet threat and appropriate ways of addressing it has widened. West European nations have definite qualms about the USSR but few of them place as extreme an interpretation on the danger or condone quite as militaristic a response as that currently adopted by the United States. The USA's European allies generally do not trust Moscow and feel that while current Soviet objectives may be defensive, a shift in the military balance away from the West could cause these objectives to be revised in a more predatory direction. The majority seems, however, to believe that military expansion in Europe and the imposition of Soviet-type governments on captive peoples do not rank very high on the Kremlin's list of priorities. To the extent that the danger is recognized, many allies tend to differ with their alliance leader—and sometimes with each other—as to how best to deal with it. Most notably, they are less likely to place as single-minded an emphasis on the build-up of armed force and tough rhetoric and are generally more prone to seek negotiations, the relaxation of tensions and even active co-operation with the Soviet Union—particularly in the economic sphere—in order to reduce the threat from that quarter. A messianic struggle against Communism is certainly not held to be a more worthy pursuit than that of detente.

If there is disagreement as to the nature of the threat within Europe itself, there are even wider differences concerning the problems originating in the Third World. European countries, unlike the USA and, in particular, the Reagan Administration, typically do not view most efforts at abrupt leftward change in Third World nations as the direct consequence of Soviet plotting and orchestration. On the contrary—as has recently been demonstrated with regard to Central America—they are far more sensitive to the socio-economic problems that breed revolutionary fervour. This comparatively sophisticated reaction, which may be the product of their own more complex social and political histories, has led to the advocacy of socio-economic, rather than purely military, solutions to the polarization and instability that afflict so many developing societies. And since the interests of most European countries in the Third World tend to be more restricted than those of the USA, a disinclination to bear significant military risks merely to accommodate the USA's extra-European objectives is entirely understandable. For example, the involvement of either Italy or Greece in a war in the Middle East featuring the superpowers—and possibly leading to nuclear combat—would run counter to just about any reasonable estimate of the national interests of these two nations.

A partial alienation of European opinion from the USA is attributable to such differences. In a survey conducted at the end of 1981, an average of 43 per cent of respondents in seven West European countries declared that they had little or no confidence in the "ability of the United States to deal responsibly with world problems".[107] Although a large proportion of the European public remains committed to the Atlantic Alliance, in five countries surveyed by the United States Information Agency the desire to leave NATO and to become a neutral country increased during President Reagan's first year in office.[108]

Thus there are pressures for change, and these pressures stem from a contradiction. On the one hand, because of the hierarchical nature of the Alliance and due to military logistics, the pursuit of external goals by the USA can affect, both directly and indirectly, the security of European allies. On the other hand, the European allies do not wholeheartedly accept this situation and emerging divergencies between Europe and the USA make the situation less acceptable than it once was. Moreover, Europe's dependence on the USA has decreased significantly since the early post-war period when the structure of allied relationships was initially established and this makes the situation even less tenable.

It is not that the security interests of the USA and various West European countries may not overlap in the Third World. Sometimes they do and this often implies that the military risks and costs must be shared. But the interests of the European nations require (*a*) that they be able to restrict their involvement in the USA's Third World ventures in such a way that they become embroiled only where their own national objectives are demonstrably at stake, and (*b*) that the risks of an overall East–West confrontation should be minimized (since few Third World goals justify the dangers to Europe of a war between the superpowers).

The room for manoeuvre is, however, limited. Some of the problems described in this study are inherent in the nature of the Atlantic Alliance, yet this alliance is authentically desired by its members as a guarantee of their security and their democratic freedoms. Policy suggestions should, thus, not be of a sort that might undermine the basic consensus behind the Western alliance or the integrity of its overall structure. Given these requirements, two lines of action suggest themselves. European nations could direct their efforts at both the political and the military levels of the problem. On the political level they might seek to dampen superpower conflicts of interest in the Third World and help to find ways of overcoming these antagonisms. And on the military level they might attempt to steer superpower military deployments in a less threatening direction and to set their own military relations with alliance leaders on a footing that would make unwanted participation in Third World clashes less likely. The two sorts of action are perfectly compatible and effective policy might require efforts on both fronts.

II. Dealing with conflicting US–Soviet policies in the Third World

What can European nations do to move East–West relations in the Third World off the path of fiercely competing interests and implacable hostility? Several possibilities come to mind but two things are evident at the very outset. To begin with, most initiatives to this effect would have to come from West European nations. The USSR's allies are not as directly involved in their superpower's Third World ventures as several of the USA's NATO partners are likely to be and it is obvious that Soviet allies enjoy very little room for independent foreign policy manoeuvres. Second, these efforts would primarily have to be directed at the USA. This is not because the USA bears more responsibility than the USSR for the state of superpower relations in the Third World—the contrary may be true—but simply because it is far easier to exert effective influence within the Atlantic Alliance than across bloc lines. The USSR is not totally impervious to pressure from the USA's friends and allies but the amount of change in its Third World policies that can be thus induced is probably minimal. Consequently, as a matter of what is pragmatically feasible, West European efforts would have to focus on their own alliance and bloc leader. What could they hope to achieve in this context? Three specific approaches could be tried.

To begin with, European nations could seek, through their own external initiatives, to remove bones of contention between the two sides or, at least, to lower the stakes of the disputes. Though little has been achieved along these lines in the past, new initiatives have recently surfaced. Second, and more modestly, the European nations could propose to the superpowers ways of dealing with their conflicts—rather than trying actually to resolve them themselves. They could, for example, try to identify facets of a problem which had escaped the antagonists. Third, they might pressure the USA—and the Kremlin if possible—to abandon pursuits which do not justify the danger of an East–West collision. (If the incompatibility cannot be resolved, some retrenchment from overly dangerous goals could be urged.) While these strategies can be distinguished logically, they would obviously overlap. The record here is not particularly impressive but neither is it entirely bleak.

Willy Brandt's conciliatory initiatives *vis-à-vis* member countries of the WTO helped to move Washington off the conventional tracks of Cold War reasoning and prepared the ground in which detente could take root for a time. Following President de Gaulle's lead, Chancellor Brandt undertook to set inter-bloc relations on a course that corresponded more authentically with Europe's own interests. Bonn signed treaties with Czechoslovakia, the GDR, Poland and the USSR and promoted the four-power treaty on Berlin in 1971 (by which Moscow officially acknowledged the link between West Berlin and the Federal Republic of Germany). The first articulations of *Ostpolitik* met with suspicion and disapproval on the part of the Nixon Administration; yet these initiatives removed certain major obstacles to better East–West relations and despite the initial misgivings of the USA, they provided the foundation for the steps towards reconciliation subsequently taken by Nixon and Brezhnev. In particular, resolving the problem of the status of Berlin removed a major stumbling block.

Nonetheless, it is one thing for FR Germany to have dealt with a problem that was directly within its own political purview; it is quite another thing to expect European governments to settle the superpowers' quarrels in the Third World—and typically this is not attempted. Some less ambitious efforts along these general lines have, however, been recorded. The European Community's attempt to promote a peace settlement for the Middle East is a case in point. While traditionally willing to let the USA take the lead in this region, the EEC's member states have more recently sought solutions on their own collective initiative. The Venice Declaration of June 1980, for example, called for a solution that would simultaneously recognize Israel's right to a secure existence and the right of the Palestinians to autonomy and would also end Israeli occupation of Arab lands. This was neither a particularly startling nor unusually bold position but it did represent an attempt to forge an independent policy for resolving an international problem which had major escalatory potential. While the causal link is admittedly speculative, President Reagan's peace plan may have owed something to the European initiative.

European governments nonetheless lack significant diplomatic and military leverage with regard to most Third World issues, even those with broad international ramifications. Since the impact of European countries on regional matters is likely to be slight even when they are willing to act independently of Washington, not too much should be expected in the way of direct action on the sources of superpower clashes in the Third World.

It is more likely that some impact can be produced in the second manner, that is by helping the superpowers to identify areas of possible compromise and co-operation rather than trying directly to resolve the issues at the root of the dispute. Since European governments do not have as much of a vested interest in the outcome of such disputes, they may frequently be in a better position to recognize the contours of an acceptable solution. They may, in other words, often be able to play a role similar to that which arbitrators sometimes perform in industrial disputes in developed societies.

The importance of this kind of function goes beyond suggesting compromises or resolutions which may have eluded the parties themselves. The superpowers are often able to identify workable solutions but are unable to act on them due to domestic political constraints and the weight of past rhetoric. In such situations, suggestions by allies, that is by nations that share the same basic values, can impart legitimacy to solutions which Washington, for example, would not have wished to propose on its own.

Such a European role may have importance not only in avoiding a US–Soviet confrontation in the first place but even in limiting the horizontal and vertical escalation of such a conflict should it nevertheless occur. For example, there were several points in our two scenarios, particularly at the commencement of hostilities, at which de-escalation would still be feasible. In the case of the Persian Gulf, this would be at the initial stage of the covert superpower struggle for influence, or even after preliminary skirmishes and regional military occupation. At these points, the USA's European allies could take the initiative of suggesting stable solutions to post-Khomeini Iran's political problems. They could even go so far as to participate in an international guarantee of that country's neutrality. In the Arab–Israeli scenario, the question of a European role could quickly become relevant since the conflict was assumed to escalate so rapidly and uncontrollably. The most important contribution in this context would be to help avert a major crisis in the first place by making an active contribution to the search for a solution to the Lebanese and Palestinian problems. The tentative activism presaged by the Venice Declaration should therefore be infused with new vigour.

If either of the two hypothetical clashes were to reach the point of actual fighting between the superpowers, the peace-making role of European governments would be reduced but could still be significant. It might, for example, be very useful to engineer 'pauses' in the escalatory process, that is, a type of firebreak during which passions could cool off, the stakes and costs of the conflict be reassessed, and tentative 'peace-feelers' proffered. The need for allied consultation might, under certain conditions, provide a credible excuse for such pauses. European nations could make a point of pressing for such consultations. At times, military imperatives will preclude such pauses but they would clearly have a potential role in checking escalation.

What of the third strategy of applying pressure where possible to induce the USA (and the USSR) to abandon the pursuit of objectives and positions that might lead to an East–West confrontation? European governments have occasionally tried to convince the United States to modify overly uncompromising positions towards the Soviet Union. Following the imposition of martial law in Poland in late 1981, for example, Washington decided to suspend its participation in the Madrid negotiations designed to supplement the Helsinki Final Act of 1974 on promoting security, co-operation and human rights in Europe. Unhappy about the US withdrawal, the West European participants persevered in trying to set the talks back on track. In response to this pressure and desiring to avoid a rift in the Atlantic Alliance, the USA agreed in November 1982 to resume the negotiations. Similarly, it was as a result of European insistence that the Reagan Administration softened its hardline stance on the transfer of pipeline equipment to the Soviet Union. These were issues of direct concern to the European nations involved. It is by no means clear that the same effects could be produced in circumstances where the interests of the European countries are less immediate and their leverage more modest.

We are led to conclude that there is some scope for a useful European role in affecting the political context within which US–Soviet confrontations in the Third World could occur. (The European nations might, for example, propose codified rules of superpower conduct in developing regions.) But such scope as may exist is strictly limited and initiatives of this sort should be complemented by policies targeted at the military level of the overall problem.

III. *Military deployments and activities*

If the military presences of the USSR and the USA in certain parts of the world increase the risk of widespread confrontations, the European nations may want to influence these presences and activities in less threatening directions. Such attempts could involve efforts to discourage the deployment of certain weapons in certain regions or to steer the superpowers away from those operations which carry the greatest threat of horizontal or vertical escalation. Not all military activities necessarily come under this heading and, from a Western point of view, the dangers of crisis instability and conflict escalation must be balanced against the objective requirements of deterrence. But though certain forms of military activity may be considered desirable, the national and collective interests of European countries require that these countries avoid situations where the dangers are not justified by their *own* stakes in the regional issues.

Two questions should then be asked. How willing are European governments to challenge US military activities which they consider unwarranted or harmful? And how much of a difference can the opinions of European governments on such issues be expected to make?

While the nations of Western Europe differ in their attitudes to these questions, few are totally unwilling to voice their disapproval of those US military ventures which they consider most ill-advised. Although criticism of the USA's engagement in Viet Nam was often muted, it was also, on occasions, quite sharp. And virtually all of the USA's European friends expressed some misgivings about the armed intervention in Grenada.

The European allies are not likely to be more circumspect in their criticism when US military activity strikes closer to home. Armed involvement by the USA in the Middle East is sometimes welcomed by European allies—as in the early phases of the multinational force in Beirut—but is also at times the object of open disapproval. And when US forces were placed on nuclear alert in October 1973, many NATO members were outraged that such a dangerous and momentous decision had not had the benefit of their prior advice.[109]

The effectiveness of European opinions and protestations has not, however, been established. Although Margaret Thatcher, one of the Reagan Administration's staunchest European supporters, had expressly pleaded against the invasion of Grenada, Washington was unswayed in its resolve to oust by force a government which it disliked. Nor have its allies managed to dissuade the USA from direct military action against Syrian positions in Lebanon. In autumn 1983, the USA undertook its largest naval build-up —including three aircraft-carrier groups—in the eastern Mediterranean. This was a scarcely veiled threat against Syria (which the USA wishes to dislodge from Lebanon). In early November, Prime Minister Thatcher expressed her government's concern about US naval activity and warned that a US decision to use force in that country would further damage relations between London and Washington.[110] At virtually the same time, the French Foreign Minister Claude Cheysson criticized the "fleet movements and singularly aggressive statements" and worried about the escalatory potential of a US attack against Syrian-backed groups.[111]

Washington appeared to be unaffected by the allies' concerns. On 4 December, 24 hours after an Israeli strike against guerrilla bases in Lebanon, 28 US fighter-bombers launched a massive aerial attack against Syrian anti-aircraft positions. Ten days later, the battleship *New Jersey* attacked Syrian missile launchers with its 16-inch guns. Other attacks followed. Despite explicitly voiced concern by two major allies, the USA extended the scope of its military activity in the Lebanon, placing itself on the brink of open warfare with Syria, the Soviet Union's principal ally in the region.

It would seem that not too much should be expected of the European governments' powers to act as a restraining influence on US military engagements abroad. The effectiveness of such an influence may vary depending on the incumbent US administration but the USA should generally be expected to follow its own counsel in these matters. Washington has its own ideas of what its external objectives call for and is unlikely to allow these ideas to be overridden by the preferences of other members of the Atlantic Alliance.

Though it is not generally possible for other members of the Alliance to influence US military deployments and operations in a less threatening direction, the allies should at least be able to arrange their military links with their alliance leader in such a way as to retain maximal control over the extent of their *own* participation in regional confrontations. Previous chapters have shown that there are major risks associated with US use of European military installations for *en route* assistance, logistic support or actual staging platforms. Such use may at times correspond to the security interests of the nations involved, but these nations should be in a position to determine the matter themselves. This in turn requires independence of two sorts.

First, the European countries should judge for themselves the merits of the regional dispute and decide whether the issues justify the risks of involvement. Second, they should maintain ultimate control, on a case-by-case basis, of the way in which their military facilities may be used by the USA. Although much information regarding base-use agreements is not public, it is evident that few European nations are willing to abdicate sovereignty in this regard.

From what has been discussed in previous chapters it would seem obvious that the two NATO countries to which such sovereignty is most crucial are Greece and Turkey. These two countries are geographically nearest to the likely theatres of operation and it is primarily, though not exclusively, through their military entanglement that the hypothesized conflicts were assumed to spread to other parts of Europe. Both nations have recently negotiated new base agreements with Washington.

Greece, under the Papandreou government, has shown a particularly strong resolve to maintain a measure of independence in political and military matters. Although it had initially threatened to withdraw from NATO and to close US bases, the government of the Panhellenic Socialist Union has retained its alliance links and obligations, prompted by fear of weakening Greece's position *vis-à-vis* Turkey. It has, nevertheless, kept its own counsel on international issues. For example, while welcoming President Reagan's Middle East peace plan, Athens has urged greater efforts to bring the PLO in as a full negotiating partner. The Papandreou government has supported proposals for a nuclear weapon-free zone in the area and the WTO's calls for a non-aggression treaty. These initiatives led the US Assistant Secretary of State for European affairs to condemn what he considered to be "still another step of Greece's departure from allied unanimity".[112]

In July 1983 the USA and Greece reached an agreement allowing the operation of US military bases in Greece for an additional five years,[113] and it can be assumed that Athens has not granted its ally a blank cheque regarding the circumstances and manner in which these facilities may be used. The

Papandreou government's past performance makes such a course unlikely. In order to avoid involvement in Lebanon's problems, for example, it has barred Italian and US aircraft from passing through Greek airspace and over territorial waters with weapons for the multinational force in Beirut. Such caution would probably extend to other non-NATO issues as well.

Turkey's stances are somewhat more muted. While the current government sees pretty much eye-to-eye with Washington on most East–West matters, it maintains an independent position on several regional issues. For instance, Turkey differs with the USA over the problems of the Middle East. It has sought close relations with moderate Arab states—to which it is bound by economic interests—and it has supported the Palestinian cause with more vigour than most other members of NATO. (Turkey, for example, supports the Fez Proposals rather than the Reagan Peace Plan as a basis for accommodation.) Ankara has also kept its distance from several US military operations. It did not, for instance, permit the USA to use its refuelling and reconnaissance facilities during the US airlift to Israel in 1973.

As explained earlier, the USA enjoys access to a number of military installations in Turkey and in March 1980 the two countries signed an Agreement for Cooperation on Defense and Economy. The document emphasized that "the extent of the defense cooperation envisaged in the Agreement shall be limited to obligations arising out of the North Atlantic Treaty".[114] The implication is that the agreement does not grant a mandate to the USA to employ these bases for out-of-area contingencies. The bases could, nonetheless, play a major role in both a Persian Gulf flare-up and a military crisis in the eastern Mediterranean. It is not clear how the Turkish government would respond to such pressures. The response would probably depend on the specifics of the situation. As one analyst has pointed out: "Turkey wants to reserve its freedom of action to stand aloof from or participating in a Gulf operation according to the circumstances of the specific case and the nature of the operation itself. This implies that Turkey might well act militarily, on the basis of an adhoc decision, against an actual threat to the Gulf".[115]

If this is an accurate statement of the Turkish position, then it is consistent with the desiderata suggested above: an autonomous ability to weigh the merits of military involvement and to act accordingly without being drawn into an undesired participation through external pressure.

In a somewhat similar vein, the Gonzales government in Spain has been seeking to define for itself an appropriate military role within NATO and in relation to the USA. Spain too strives to maintain good relations with the Arab world and is concerned about the possibility of its airbases being used by USCENTCOM in the event of a conflict in the Persian Gulf or the eastern Mediterranean. Negotiations on US military bases in Spain led to an agreement that was signed by both governments. The full text has not been made public but it has been reported that "it includes a formula allowing Madrid some latitude to decide, case by case, on the use of the bases which are technically Spanish but actually under American control".[116]

It is not at all clear what "some latitude" really means. When the new Socialist Prime Minister, Felipe Gonzales, took office late in 1982 he urged a renegotiation of the pact since it was based on the assumption that Spain was integrated into NATO's military command. Although Spain did join NATO in May 1982, the Gonzales government has indicated a preference for following France in not adhering to the actual military structure. The French case suggests that this is a viable position for certain countries.

These examples lead to the conclusion that European nations, particularly those most vulnerable to early involvement in the regional confrontations of the superpowers, appear resolved to maintain as much control as possible over the extent of their participation; at least with regard to the use of military facilities on their soil. It may, in any case, be easier for them to stay out of such conflicts by withholding direct or logistic support of certain types than to help avert the conflict in the first place. But as our scenarios suggest, the dynamics of conflict could come to override the military decisions of European governments. There are, moreover, circumstances in which *some* level of engagement would be consistent with the countries' own interests although involvement at higher levels would not be. For example, there are circumstances under which a nation would wish to participate in limited conventional operations in order to deter or fend off a threat to Western security, but would consider the threat of a nuclear exchange quite unacceptable. It is thus important to consider not only possible ways of avoiding combat involvement in the first place, but also means of controlling the vertical escalation of fighting should conflict nevertheless occur on European soil. In particular, methods of avoiding embroilment in a *nuclear* war should be considered.

In outlining the scenarios, some points at which combat could cross the nuclear threshold were indicated. The scenarios do not exhaust the full gamut of possibilities but it seems most likely that nuclear weapons might be used in three areas: the Balkans, northern Europe and central Europe. The Balkans would be vulnerable at a very early stage of the confrontation. In the event of a Persian Gulf conflict, Turkish involvement could occur at the very beginning of US combat operations. Turkey is an obvious staging post for USCENTCOM interventions in the area and would in any case probably be asked to provide some logistic support for the US military effort. Several paths could lead the parties over the nuclear precipice.

If the Soviet Union decided to take direct military action against military installations in Turkey for pre-emptive or retaliatory purposes, it might rely on its SS-20 missiles or on nuclear-equipped Backfire bombers for escalation control. If Soviet theatre nuclear forces were placed in a high state of alert, the USA might deem it prudent to pre-empt, using its own nuclear weapons, most probably cruise missiles. Obviously this would be a highly escalatory move from the US point of view and is, perhaps, not a very likely contingency. But as the military dynamics of the crisis come into play it could not be dismissed.

Another possible development is that US *tactical* nuclear weapons could be used to repel a Soviet conventional thrust into Turkey. If it seemed impossible to stop the Soviet invasion with conventional forces, or if it appeared that nuclear storage depots at Erzurum (always assuming that they exist) would be overrun, it is hard to imagine that these weapons would not be used. Similar risks are associated with a naval conflict in the eastern Mediterranean produced by an Arab–Israeli war. If the USSR invaded Turkish Thrace in order to gain control of the Dardanelles and the Bosphorus, attempts to counter them could go beyond the use of conventional forces alone. Nuclear storage depots seem, moreover, to exist on Greek territory as well. If Turkey was drawn into a conflict, Greek participation would be virtually inevitable and the risks of nuclear warfare would increase accordingly.

The northern flank could also be a flashpoint of nuclear conflict if war occurred in either the Middle East or the Persian Gulf. In one hypothesis of horizontal escalation, the USA would seek to compensate for losses in the original combat theatres by counter-offensives against Soviet positions in northern areas. An associated aim might be to deny Soviet attack submarines and SSBNs access to the Atlantic. Under these conditions, naval combat between the two sides would be a real possibility. It is difficult, moreover, to see how Norway could stay out of the fighting since its military facilities would be required for the support of US operations and possible ground attacks against Soviet positions on the Kola Peninsula. Norwegian territory would almost certainly be implicated in the fighting and this could rapidly escalate to the tactical nuclear level.

While nuclear conflict could come to central Europe as a result of horizontal spread, it could also occur directly. If both the southern and northern flanks of the continent were parties to an East–West conflict, the stakes of war would have attained a level where either superpower might anticipate an assault against its interests in central Europe. If, for example, this involved a Soviet drive into the Federal Republic of Germany, a tactical nuclear response is entirely conceivable—with the possibility of escalation to theatre-nuclear and strategic warfare.

Several parts of Europe could thus fall victim to nuclear combat even if the US–Soviet flare-up were to originate elsewhere. Given this possibility, it is essential to reduce the likelihood of vertical escalation as much as possible. One promising way of achieving this is to establish nuclear weapon-free zones (NWFZ) in those areas where the nuclear threshold is most likely to be breached. There have been proposals to this end and the general parameters of such zones can be discerned.

A NWFZ would entail an obligation on the part of the nations whose territories it covered not to possess nuclear weapons on their soil. It would also commit them to prohibit such deployments on their territory by other nations, as well as the transit of such weapons through this territory to the extent possible. These obligations would apply both in peace and war. States possessing nuclear weapons, particularly the superpowers, would be bound to respect the status of the zones. They would, furthermore, promise neither to use nor to threaten to use nuclear weapons against the states of the zone. They would, in fact, provide 'negative security guarantees'.

Antarctica and much of Latin America (by the Treaty of Tlatelolco) approach the status of a NWFZ. Such zones would clearly be desirable in certain parts of Europe as well. Their establishment has at times been suggested. Bulgaria, Greece, Romania and Yugoslavia have, on several occasions, proposed that a nuclear weapon-free zone be established in the Balkans.[117] While Turkey's position within NATO causes it to be circumspect in this regard, it is likely that Ankara would also see the merits of such proposals. A Balkan NWFZ could be expected to encompass these five countries and, ideally, Albania as well. The zone might include local waters between longitudes 15° and 30°E and latitudes 35° and 45°N. It would thus cover virtually the entire Adriatic, the Aegean Sea and relevant portions of the eastern Mediterranean.

Such a zone would not materially affect NATO's ability to deter a Soviet threat to the region. Of approximately 6 000 US tactical nuclear weapons in Europe, only a very small fraction are, in fact, stored in Greece and Turkey. Neither country, moreover, has delivery systems which could place significant portions of the USSR within range of those nuclear weapons that are stored on their soil. Nor would nuclear weapons deployed in local waters be essential to deterrence. Thus the need to discourage aggressive designs on the region cannot justify the risks of crisis instability and vertical escalation created by the presence of these weapons.

The idea of a nuclear weapon-free zone in the Nordic area has also received a fair amount of attention.[118] It was enunciated by President Kekkonen of Finland as early as 1963 and was later endorsed by the Swedish government. Sweden also proposed that the zone should include weapons "which are intended for targets within the zone, are stationed near the zone, and have ranges of a scale which makes them best suited for targets within the Nordic area".[119] The point is that areas adjacent to the zone as narrowly defined, such as the Leningrad Military District, the Norwegian Sea and the Barents Sea, should also be covered by the provisions of the arrangement. It would, in other words, not imply a unilateral decision to forgo nuclear weapons on the part of the West.

Although it may be fanciful to expect that the whole of central Europe could be made into a NWFZ in the near future, a somewhat less ambitious goal is realistic and would be beneficial. Specifically, it may be possible to avoid placing nuclear weapons in the most sensitive regions of central Europe. These are the areas that would immediately be swept into conventional conflict and where both the possibility of tactical nuclear combat and theatre nuclear pre-emption are high. An early proposal by the Polish Foreign Minister Rapacki in 1957 would have had Poland, Czechoslovakia, the GDR and the FRG agree neither to produce or deploy nuclear weapons within their borders. Considered little more than a Soviet ploy at the time, the Rapacki Plan evoked little enthusiasm in the West. More recently, the so-called Palme Commission put forward a more modest and workable plan.[120] This would involve a strip of 150 km on each side of the border between FR Germany on the one side and the GDR and Czechoslovakia on the other—precisely the areas where fighting would be most likely to begin—within which nuclear weapons might not be placed. Adherence to this obligation would be monitored by on-site inspection, a matter which should not raise serious feasibility problems if an agreement were to be reached. The point of such a nuclear disengagement zone would be to avoid the likelihood that a conventional clash in central Europe would rapidly escalate to a nuclear confrontation, that is, before diplomacy has had a proper chance to terminate the conflict. Again, deterrence should not be weakened under these conditions since Soviet territory would still be within range of weapons deployed outside the zone. The incentive to employ tactical nuclear weapons in a 'use them or lose them' mode at the outset of the fighting would, on the other hand, be substantially reduced.

Not only would it be useful to remove nuclear weapons from such a zone, but also certain categories of heavy conventional weaponry, particularly as current conventional postures could make pre-emptive, and initially non-nuclear, strikes more likely. Soviet force postures have traditionally stressed offensive thrusts westwards if conflict were to break out (or appeared imminent and unavoidable). More recently, US Airland Battle doctrine and the development of deep-strike technologies have implied an offensive posture for Washington as well. Regulation of conventional forces in central Europe could, therefore, decrease the incentive to pre-empt (before falling victim to the adversary's offensive strikes) and make it less likely that political or military crises would trigger conflict in central Europe.

Clearly there is nothing particularly novel about these proposals. However, in addition to the merits with which they are habitually credited, they also promise to lower the potential costs within Europe of the superpowers' extra-European conflicts. There was always a good case to be made for nuclear weapon-free zones and nuclear disengagement zones. The case is even stronger when placed in this broader context.

IV. Final thoughts

Three broad strategies have been proposed in this chapter: (*a*) foreign-policy initiatives to reduce the likelihood of US–Soviet conflicts in the Third World; (*b*) controlling the military synapses (especially the military bases and logistical links) through which the European states could be drawn into these clashes; and (*c*) measures to prevent the nuclearization of those conflicts that do spread to the European continent. The first of these strategies addresses the political level of the overall problem while the second and third concern the military level. Each of the strategies faces significant obstacles and assumes a substantial effort. Success will partially depend on circumstances beyond European control but also on the amount of common effort mustered on behalf of these objectives.

Clearly, there are differences in specific aspects of the national interests of various European nations as well as in their perceptions of international problems. But the successful pursuit of the general goals proposed here would require an articulated, collective policy. This, in turn, may call for an appropriate institutional framework—one which facilitates regular communication and co-ordination as well as the generation of expert information and which would ensure the implementation of agreed policies. In addition to providing a setting through which broadly defined objectives could be pursued, at least one other valuable function could be performed by such an organization. If unwarranted involvement in superpower conflicts is to be avoided, it may be necessary to decide collectively, and in advance, which circumstances would justify participation of a certain sort and which would not. On the basis of these decisions, measures would be designed, corresponding to the anticipated phases of potential confrontations, to avoid undesired forms of participation. Collective means of implementing these measures would be devised. The point is that European nations are more likely to be engulfed by conflicts whose contours they had not anticipated and for which they had not planned their responses in advance. Plausible and clear scenarios of the sequences of events which could threaten European security are thus required. These analyses and decisions could be produced in the proper organizational context by a competent staff.

Several proposals have been made, albeit for different reasons, for institutions to supplement traditional NATO structures and to encourage a more powerful European voice on out-of-area issues. The directors of the Councils or Institutes for International Relations of the USA, UK, France and FR Germany have recently suggested that the seven-nation summits be accorded more of a role in decisions of this sort.[121] (They have also suggested that a small but permanent secretariat be established for this purpose.) More significantly still, they advocate the establishment of groups of 'principal nations' to accept concrete responsibilities in various troubled areas. These 'principle nations' would typically be the USA, UK, France, FR Germany and Japan. Their purpose would be to engage in joint assessment of the situation and crisis management. The idea behind this is that, since these nations make a greater contribution to the defence of Western interests outside the NATO area, the USA would take their viewpoints more genuinely into account in this framework.

Pieter Dankert, president of the European Parliament, has argued that serious differences between the USA and Western Europe "will only be resolved if and when West Europeans provide their own assessments of security issues in a collective and coherent manner". He proposes that the

Eurogroup within NATO, augmented by France—that is the Independent European Program Group (IEPG)—could be used towards this end (as well as informal caucuses of the European members of NATO).[122]

Each of the proposals has shortcomings from the perspective of the objectives advanced in this chapter. The seven-nation summits are not exclusively European and are, in any case, designed primarily for the discussion of economic matters. The 'principal nations' approach appears too *ad hoc* to establish a foundation for the sort of goals that have been suggested. The IEPG deals essentially with various aspects of arms production and trade and may not be competent to deal with more ambitious tasks. It would seem a far better idea to establish a new structure than to graft new functions onto old structures or to pursue fluid and *ad hoc* solutions. Concerned governments could beneficially devote some thought to the matter. None of these proposals should undermine the bonds between the USA and Western Europe. The proposals are, rather, designed to adapt Atlantic relations to evolving political realities and to the changing nature of threats to European security.

Eastern Europe may also have a role to play. While the Soviet Union's allies are not as directly involved in the issues we have been discussing here, and although their freedom of action is more restricted than that of the European democracies, they too have responsibilities. Improved relations with the West have given the countries of Eastern Europe a vested interest in blocking the further deterioration of superpower relations and in encouraging the movement back towards detente. Since US–Soviet relations in the Third World have so great an impact on the overall tone of East–West relations, the USSR's allies would benefit by putting pressure on their alliance leader to steer away from provocative behaviour in the Third World. Their leverage in this respect is modest but not, presumably, wholly non-existent. NWFZs and nuclear disengagement zones require, moreover, the co-operation of several members of the WTO: Romania and Bulgaria have endorsed the idea of a nuclear weapon-free zone in the Balkan region; a nuclear disengagement zone in central Europe would obviously require the participation of the German Democratic Republic and Czechoslovakia.

For all these proposals there is an intellectually necessary point of departure: the realization that cataclysmic experiences can result from what do not appear to be major causes. Events and activities which, from the perspective of many European countries, may seem peripheral to their central concerns, can have very substantial consequences for their future security. Rivalry between the USA and the USSR in the Third World is a case in point.

Notes and references

1. Whiting, A., *China Crosses the Yalu: The Decision to Enter the Korean Wars* (Stanford University Press, Stanford, 1960).
2. See Hosmer, S. T. and Wolfe, T. W., *Soviet Policy and Practice toward Third World Conflicts* (D. C. Heath, Lexington, 1983), especially chapter 1.
3. Quoted in LaFeber, W., *America, Russia, and the Cold War 1945–1975*, 3rd edition (John Wiley, New York, 1976), p. 235.
4. A good discussion of the BPA is provided in George, A. L., 'The Basic Principles Agreement of 1972: origins and expectations', *Managing U.S.–Soviet Rivalry: Problems of Crisis Prevention*, edited by A. L. George (Westview, Boulder, 1983), pp. 107–118.
5. Deporte, A. W., *Europe between the Superpowers: The Enduring Balance* (Yale University Press, New Haven, 1979), p. 157.
6. See 'Germans bracing for Soviet move', *The New York Times*, 24 October 1962; 'Cuban crisis weighing heavily on minds of calm Berliners', *The New York Times*, 26 October 1962; 'Allies in Berlin bolster forces', *The New York Times*, 26 October 1962; 'Bonn acts again to bolster arms', *The New York Times*, 30 October 1962.
7. 'Relief felt in NATO at Cuban relaxation', *The New York Times*, 26 October 1962.
8. According to LaFeber (note 3), p. 192.
9. United States Joint Chiefs of Staff, *United States Military Posture, Fiscal Year 1984* (US Government Printing Office, Washington, D.C., 1983), p. 3.
10. US Joint Chiefs of Staff (note 9), p. 5.
11. US Department of Defense, *Report of the Secretary of Defense Caspar W. Weinberger to the Congress, Fiscal Year 1984* (US Government Printing Office, Washington, D.C., 1983), p. 52.
12. 'Pentagon draws up first strategy for fighting a long nuclear war', *The New York Times*, 30 May 1982. See also 'Aide says U.S. policy is to "prevail" over Russians', *The New York Times*, 17 June 1982. Probably due to the disquieted public reactions to reports of this plan the terms 'prevailing' and 'protracted nuclear war' were removed in 1983 in the directive entitled *Fiscal Year 1985–89 Defense Guidance*. On this latter change see 'New Weinberger directive redefines military policy', *The New York Times*, 22 March 1983.
13. An excellent discussion of the concept of escalation dominance is provided in Jervis, R., 'The madness beyond MAD: escalation dominance and current U.S. strategic policy', unpublished manuscript, January 1983.

14. The 'defense guidance plan' as reported in *The New York Times*, 30 May 1982 (note 12).

15. Examples of this trend towards dual capabilities are numerous. F-4 Phantom aircraft in the Marine Air–Ground Task Force with a solely conventional capacity are being replaced by F-18 Hornets that are certified for the delivery of nuclear munitions. Nuclear-capable AV-8B jumbo jets are replacing non-nuclear AV-8As. Non-nuclear 105-mm howitzers are giving way to dual-capable 155-mm guns. Army and Marine 8-inch howitzers will be equipped to fire 'neutron' warheads, etc. See Paine, C., 'Reagatomics, or how to "prevail"', *The Nation*, 25 May 1983, pp. 423–31.

16. This is the so-called TLAM-N cruise missile described in Kaplan, M., 'U.S. cruise missile programs', *Arms Control Today*, May 1983. See also Paine (note 15), pp. 427–28.

17. *International Energy Statistical Review* (Central Intelligence Agency, Washington, D.C., 30 August 1983).

18. For example, the US Congressional Budget Office has estimated that the loss of Saudi Arabian oil alone for one year would cost the USA $272 billion and increase the inflation rate by 20 per cent. See Nye, J. S., 'Energy and security', *Energy and Security*, edited by D. A. Deese and J. S. Nye (Ballinger, Cambridge, 1981), p. 3.

19. Much of the following discussion draws on *US Minerals Dependence on South Africa*, Committee on Foreign Relations, US Senate (US Government Printing Office, Washington, D.C., 1982); *Imports of Minerals from South Africa by the United States and the O.E.C.D. Countries*, Congressional Research Service (Library of Congress, Washington, D.C., 1981).

20. *Prospects for Soviet Oil Production* (Central Intelligence Agency, Washington, D.C., April 1977).

21. See, for example, *Allocation of Resources in the Soviet Union and China—1981*, Joint Economic Committee, US Congress (US Government Printing Office, Washington, D.C., 1981), pp. 81–111. See also Hardt, J. P., 'Soviet and East European energy supplies' in Franssen, H. *et al.*, *World Energy Supply and International Security* (Institute for Foreign Policy Analysis, Cambridge, 1983), pp. 28–64.

22. Quoted in Shafer, M., 'Mineral myths', *Foreign Policy*, Summer 1982, p. 154.

23. See also the discussion in Papp, D. S., 'Soviet non-fuel mineral resources: surplus or scarcity?' *Resources Policy*, September 1982, pp. 155–76.

24. A good discussion of the geopolitics of maritime shipping lanes is provided in Moodie, M. and Cottrel, A. J., *Geopolitics and Maritime Power* (Sage, Beverly Hills, 1981).

25. For descriptions see *Strategic Survey 1980–81* (International Institute for Strategic Studies, London, 1981), pp. 17–19; *Challenges for U.S. National Security: A Preliminary Report*, Part 2 (Carnegie Endowment for International Peace, Washington, D.C., 1981), pp. 165–96; US Department of Defense, *Report of the Secretary of Defense Caspar W. Weinberger to the Congress, Fiscal Year 1984* (US Government Printing Office, Washington, D.C., 1983); and Record, J., *The Rapid Deployment Force* (Institute for Foreign Policy Analysis, Cambridge, 1981).

26. These facilities are described in 'US to press for Oman, Kenya and Somalia outposts', *The New York Times*, 10 January 1980; 'U.S. experts to study new military

sites on Indian Ocean', *The New York Times*, 11 January 1980; 'U.S. naval buildup is challenging Soviet advances in Asia and Africa', *The New York Times*, 19 April 1981.

27. See 'Bright star in the desert', *Army*, February 1982, pp. 38–40.

28. Soviet force-projection capabilities are described in *Strategic Survey 1980–81* (note 25), pp. 20–21; *Challenges for U.S. National Security: A Preliminary Report* (note 25), pp. 137–38; Gormley, D. M., 'The direction and pace of Soviet force projection capabilities', *Survival*, November/December 1982, pp. 266–76.

29. This information is given in Gormley (note 28), p. 274.

30. 'Soviet is building new Afghan bases', *The New York Times*, 14 November 1982. The two major airfields are at Kandahar and Shindand.

31. *The New York Times*, 19 April 1981.

32. See note 31.

33. Arkin, W. *et al.*, 'Nuclearisation of the oceans', *Symposium on the Denuclearisation of the Oceans*, Norrtälje, Sweden, May 1984 (Myrdal Foundation, Stockholm, 1984), p. 34.

34. A description of rival superpower arms deliveries to the Middle East is provided in Pierre, A. J., *The Global Politics of Arms Sales* (Princeton University Press, Princeton, 1982).

35. Zumwalt Jr, E. R., *On Watch: A Memoir* (Times Books, New York, 1976), p. 446.

36. This information is given in US Department of Defense (note 25), p. 203.

37. Moodie and Cottrel (note 24), p. 60.

38. This is discussed in Moodie and Cottrel (note 24), pp. 59–60.

39. *The New York Times*, 19 April 1981.

40. *Challenges for U.S. National Security* (note 25), p. 133.

41. See the discussions in Moodie and Cottrel (note 24), pp. 48–50.

42. See, for example, the discussions in *NATO Today: The Alliance in Evolution, A Report to the Committee on Foreign Relations*, US Senate (US Government Printing Office, Washington, D.C., 1982); *Soviet Policy and United States Response in the Third World*, Congressional Research Service (Library of Congress, Washington, D.C., 1982), especially chapter 4.

43. 'Recent developments in East–West trade', *Economic Bulletin for Europe*, Vol. 33, No. 4, 1981.

44. For a description of recent trends see Harris, S., 'East–West economic relations: a longer term perspective', *OECD Observer*, May 1984.

45. 'Japanese to study guarding sea lane', *The New York Times*, 24 January 1983. See also Barang, M., ' "Déploiment flexible" et coopération accrue des alliés', *Le Monde Diplomatique*, March 1983.

46. *The New York Times*, 11 May 1981.

47. Quoted in *NATO Today: The Alliance in Evolution* (note 42).

48. *NATO Today: The Alliance in Evolution* (note 42), pp. 37–38.

49. This is described in Wittman, G. H., 'Political and military background for France's intervention capability', *A.E.I. Foreign Policy and Defense Review*, Vol. 4, No. 1, 1982, pp. 12–17.

50. Wittman (note 49), p. 16.

51. Perry, C., *The West, Japan and Cape Route Imports: The Oil and Mineral Trades* (Institute for Foreign Policy Analysis, Cambridge, Mass., 1982).

52. *NATO Today: The Alliance in Evolution* (note 42), p. 38. See also *Soviet Policy and*

United States Response in the Third World (note 42), pp. 245–50.

53. Quoted in 'NATO backs U.S. operations in Mideast', *The New York Times*, 3 December 1982.

54. US Department of Defense, *Report of the Secretary of Defense Caspar W. Weinberger to the Congress, Fiscal Year 1985* (US Government Printing Office, Washington, D.C., 1984).

55. *NATO Today: The Alliance in Evolution* (note 42), p. 39.

56. The missions that could be served by military installations in the Azores are described in some detail in *United States Foreign Policy Objectives and Overseas Military Installations*, Congressional Research Service (US Government Printing Office, Washington, D.C., 1979), pp. 52–53.

57. *United States Foreign Policy Objectives and Overseas Military Installations* (note 56), p. 54.

58. The discussion of US facilities in Turkey and Greece is based on *Turkey, Greece and NATO: The Strained Alliance, A Staff Report to the Committee on Foreign Relations*, US Senate (US Government Printing Office, Washington, D.C., 1980).

59. *Turkey, Greece and NATO: The Strained Alliance* (note 58), p. 9.

60. These involve air bases in Erzumurum, Batman and Mus. See 'Ankara confirme la modernization des bases aériennes mais dément un accord avec les Etats-Unis et la Turquie', *Le Monde*, 11 November 1982 and 'Accord entre les Etats-Unis et la Turquie', *Le Monde*, 11 September 1982.

61. See note 58.

62. US Department of Defense, *Report of the Secretary of Defense Caspar W. Weinberger to the Congress, Fiscal Year 1983* (US Government Printing Office, Washington, D.C., 1982), p. I-14.

63. US Department of Defense (note 62), p. I-16.

64. US Department of Defense (note 62), p. I-16.

65. US Department of Defense (note 62), p. I-16.

66. Holist, J. J., 'Norway's search for a Nordpolitik', *Foreign Affairs*, Vol. 60, No. 1, Fall 1981, p. 66.

67. A good discussion of this possibility is to be found in Miller, S. E. 'The military context: the northern seas in Soviet and American strategy', *Nuclear Disengagement in Europe*, edited by S. Lodgaard and M. Thee (Taylor & Francis, London, 1983), pp. 117–38 [a SIPRI book].

68. Miller (note 67), p. 128.

69. 'New scramble for Africa', *The Economist*, 19 September 1981.

70. Legum, C., 'Angola and the Horn of Africa' in Kaplan, S. S., *Diplomacy of Power* (The Brookings Institution, Washington, D.C., 1981), p. 622.

71. 'Soviet general says entire bloc is ready to fight in Afghanistan', *The New York Times*, 12 April 1980.

72. See Remington, R., *The Warsaw Pact* (MIT Press, Cambridge, 1971), p. 138.

73. On this issue see Volgyes, I., *The Political Reliability of the Warsaw Pact Armies* (Duke Press, Durham, 1982).

74. On the issue of Cuban involvement in Africa see, *inter alia*, Gavshon, A., *Crisis in Africa: Battleground of East and West* (Penguin Books, New York, 1981), particularly chapters 5, 10 and 11.

75. On the basis of Gormley (note 28), p. 271.

76. See Kaplan (note 70), p. 621.

77. A good discussion of Soviet risk-taking behaviour with special reference to the Persian Gulf is provided in Ross, D., 'Considering Soviet threats to the Persian Gulf', *International Security*, Vol. 6, No. 2, Fall 1981, pp. 159–80.

78. On this point see Eilts, H. F., 'Security consideration in the Persian Gulf', *International Security*, Vol. 5, No. 2, Fall 1980, especially pp. 98–99. See also Goldberg, J., 'How stable is Saudi Arabia?' *The Washington Quarterly*, Spring 1982, pp. 157–63.

79. 'A world at war', *The Defense Monitor*, Vol. 12, no. 1, 1983, p. 7.

80. Declaratory strategy on the use of conventional force is left rather open-ended. For example, the US Secretary of Defense has stated that:

> Regional internal instabilities and intraregional conflicts provide frequent opportunities for Soviet intervention through proxy state or Soviet backed sympathizers. In most cases, we would respond indirectly through economic, technical, political, or security assistance programs, depending on political conditions. U.S. military participation could range from the provision of training material, and security assistance to support for the employment of third-party assistance or the *tailored use of military force*, [emphasis added] as appropriate.

US Department of Defense, *Report of Secretary of Defense Caspar W. Weinberger to the Congress, Fiscal Year 1984* (US Government Printing Office, Washington, D.C., 1983).

81. This is described in Collins, J. M., *U.S.–Soviet Military Balance, Book VI. Far East, Middle East Assessments*, Congressional Research Service (US Government Printing Office, Washington, D.C., July 1980), pp. 90–91.

82. The difficulties are described in Epstein, J. M., 'Soviet vulnerabilities and the R.D.F. deterrent', *International Security*, Vol. 6, No. 2, Fall 1981, pp. 126–58.

83. The Soviet Union has, indeed, twice attempted to install a pro-Soviet regime in Azerbaijan: once after World War I and the second time during World War II. The logistics of occupation may, furthermore, not be overly difficult. The recent electrification of the rail link between Dhzulfa in Soviet Azerbaijan and Tabriz (Iranian Azerbaijan), for example, will make transportation between the two Azerbaijans easier than between Tehran and Tabriz. See Eilts (note 78), p. 84.

84. On this point see Westwood, J. T., 'The Soviet Union and the southern sea route', *Naval War College Review*, January/February 1982, pp. 54–66.

85. Assistant Secretary of Defense Francis West has suggested that a US campaign against Soviet shipping would be an appropriate response to Soviet aggression in the Persian Gulf. See West Jr, F., 'NATO: common boundaries for common interests', *Naval War College Review*, January/February 1981, p. 65.

86. Cordesman, A. H., 'Oman: guardian of the eastern gulf', *Armed Forces Journal International*, June 1983, p. 30.

87. See, for example, Jampoler, A. C. A., 'America's vital interests', *United States Naval Institute Proceedings*, January 1981, p. 32.

88. We are assuming, perhaps optimistically, that if a new Berlin crisis had been engineered by the USSR in stage II, it would not have developed into warfare by this time.

89. A major danger stems from the fact that the US Navy might not be able to distinguish adequately between Soviet SSNs and SSBNs. On this point see Posen, B. R., 'Inadvertent nuclear war? Escalation and NATO's northern flank', *International Security*, Vol. 7, No. 2, Fall 1982, pp. 3–27.

90. See Roberts, S. S., 'Superpower naval confrontations', *Soviet Naval Diplomacy*,

edited by B. Dismukes and J. McConnell (Pergamon Press, New York, 1979), pp. 158–221; Jabber, P. and Kolkowicz, R., 'The Arab–Israeli wars of 1967 and 1973', *Diplomacy of Power: Soviet Armed Forces as a Political Instrument*, edited by S. S. Kaplan (The Brookings Institute, Washington, D.C., 1981), pp. 412–68; Howe, J. J. T., *Multicrisis: Sea Power and Global Politics in the Missile Age* (MIT Press, Cambridge, Mass., 1971).

91. 'U.S. positioning 2,000 marines off Beirut coast', *The New York Times*, 2 September 1983.

92. The USSR had pointedly threatened Israel in 1967, 1973 and 1982 but did nothing to back up these threats. Furthermore, as the USSR undertook a sealift and airlift of equipment to its Arab clients in 1973, several Soviet planes were damaged on the ground and the merchant ship *Ilya Mechnikov* was sunk while lying at anchor in the port of Tartus in Syria. No Soviet retaliation followed. Even when, in July 1982, the Israeli invading force in Lebanon briefly occupied a consulate building inside the Soviet embassy compound in Beirut, the USSR did not respond significantly.

93. See McConnell, J. M., 'The rules of the game: a theory on the practice of super-power naval diplomacy' in Dismukes and McConnell (note 90), chapter 7.

94. For example, US success at inducing Israel to relax its pressure on Egypt's Third Army facilitated the termination of the Six Day War.

95. The nature and functions of the Sixth Fleet are described in Crow Jr, W. J., 'Allied defense of the southern region: a commander's perspective', *NATO's Sixteen Nations*, June/July 1983, pp. 18–25. See also Shear, H. E., 'The southern flank of NATO', *NATO's Fifteen Nations*, December 1978/January 1979, pp. 23–26.

96. See Vego, M., 'Soviet naval presence in the Mediterranean since 1973', *Navy International*, July 1983, pp. 424–33.

97. Soviet land-based aircraft would probably not have much of a role in the pre-emptive strike. Large numbers of aircraft taking off from Black Sea bases would give NATO advance warning of the strike and, in any case, they might not get through Greek and Turkish air defences.

98. Robert, S. S., 'The Turkish Straits and Soviet naval operations', *Navy International*, October 1981, pp. 581–85. Turner, N., 'Naval control of the Turkish Straits', *N.A.T.O.s Fifteen Nations*, Special edition 2, 1982, pp. 13–16.

99. Papas, N., 'The importance of the Hellenic navy in southern Europe operations', *N.A.T.O.s Fifteen Nations*, Special edition 2, 1982, pp. 48–51. It should be noted in this regard that the Chief of the Hellenic Navy General Staff is also Commander Eastern Mediterranean (COMEDEAST) in the NATO chain of command.

100. There has been some speculation that Backfire bombers might be based in Libya. 'A Soviet naval peril: bases in Libya', *The New York Times*, 31 January 1981, p. 11.

101. Robert (note 98), p. 584.

102. France has indeed been stressing its NATO bonds with more vigour than usual in recent years.

103. See, for example, Parker, T. W., 'Theater nuclear warfare and the U.S. navy', *Navy War College Review*, January/February 1982, pp. 3–15; Brooks, L. F., 'Tactical nuclear weapons: the forgotten face of naval war', *United States Naval Proceedings*, January 1980, pp. 29–33.

104. Parker (note 103), p. 14. The essay was awarded the Admiral Richard G. Colbert Memorial Prize.
105. US Congressional Budget Office, 'Building a 600-ship navy; timing and alternative approaches', Washington, D.C., March 1982, p. 17.
106. Quoted in Arkin (note 33), p. 7.
107. Schneider. W., 'Elite and public opinion: the alliance's new fissure?' *Public Opinion*, February/March 1983, p. 5.
108. Schneider (note 107), p. 5.
109. See, for example, Barnet, R., *The Alliance: America–Europe–Japan, Makers of the Postwar World* (Simon and Schuster, New York, 1983).
110. 'U.S. is cautioned by Mrs. Thatcher', *The New York Times*, 8 November 1983.
111. 'France, without citing the U.S., expresses concern about Mideast', *The New York Times*, 9 November 1983.
112. 'U.S. resumes talks on bases in Greece', *The New York Times*, 20 March 1983.
113. 'U.S. reaches pact on bases in Greece', *The New York Times*, 16 July 1983.
114. See the discussion in Karaosmanoglu, A. L., 'Turkey's security', *Foreign Affairs*, Vol. 62, Fall 1983, pp. 157–75.
115. Karaosmanoglu (note 114), p. 168.
116. 'U.S. military pact in trouble in Spain', *The New York Times*, 7 October 1982.
117. See Rydell, R. J. and Platias, A., 'The Balkans: a weapon-free zone', *The Bulletin of Atomic Scientists*, Vol. 38, May 1982, pp. 57–60.
118. See Lodgaard, S. and Berg, P., 'Nordic initiatives for a nuclear weapon-free zone in Europe', in SIPRI, *World Armaments and Disarmament, SIPRI Yearbook 1982* (Taylor & Francis, London, 1982), pp. 75–96.
119. Lodgaard and Berg (note 118), p. 83.
120. Independent Commission on Disarmament and Security Issues, *Common Security: A Blueprint for Survival* (Simon and Schuster, New York, 1982).
121. Kaiser, K. *et al., Western Security: What has Changed? What Should be Done?* (Council on Foreign Relations, New York, 1981).
122. Dankert, P., 'Europe together, America apart', *Foreign Policy*, Winter 1983–84, pp. 18–34.

Index

Recent and forthcoming SIPRI books published by Taylor & Francis

World Armaments and Disarmament, SIPRI Yearbook 1985
ISBN 0 85066 297 4. ISSN 0347-2205. c. 600 pp. 1985.

World Armaments and Disarmament, SIPRI Yearbooks 1978–84

The Arms Race and Arms Control 1985
ISBN 0 85066 298 2. ISSN 0265-1807. c. 200 pp. 1985.

Policies for Common Security
ISBN 0 85066 301 6. 256 pp. 1985.

No-First-Use
Edited by Frank Blackaby, Jozef Goldblat and Sverre Lodgaard
ISBN 0 85066 260 5 pbk, 0 85066 274 5 hbk. 152 pp. 1984.

Nuclear Disengagement in Europe
Edited by Sverre Lodgaard and Marek Thee
ISBN 0 85066 244 3. 272 pp. 1983.

Safeguarding the Atom: A Critical Appraisal
By David Fischer and Paul Szasz, edited by Jozef Goldblat
ISBN 0 85066 306 7. c. 250 pp. 1985.

Non-proliferation: The Why and the Wherefore
Edited by Jozef Goldblat
ISBN 0 85066 304 0. c. 400 pp. 1985.

Effects of Chemical Warfare: A Selective Review and Bibliography of British State Papers. SIPRI Chemical and Biological Warfare Studies, No. 1
By Andy Thomas
ISBN 0 85066 307 5. ISSN 0267-2357. 126 pp. 1985.

Chemical Warfare Arms Control: A Framework for Considering Policy Alternatives. SIPRI Chemical and Biological Warfare Studies, No. 2
By Julian Perry Robinson
ISBN 0 85066 308 3. ISSN 0267-2537. c. 120 pp. 1985.

The Detoxification and Natural Degradation of Chemical Warfare Agents. SIPRI Chemical and Biological Studies, No. 3
By Ralf Trapp
ISBN 0 85066 309 1. ISSN 0267-2537. c. 100 pp. 1985.

Explosive Remnants of War: Mitigating the Environmental Effects
Edited by Arthur H. Westing
ISBN 0 85066 303 2. c. 250 pp. 1985.

Environmental Warfare: ̶
Edited by Arthur H. We̶
ISBN 0 85066 278 8. 108 ̶

Herbicides in War: The L̶
Edited by Arthur H. We̶
ISBN 0 85066 265 6. 210 ̶

Space Weapons — The A̶
Edited by Bhupendra Ja̶
ISBN 0 85066 262 1. 256 ̶

Countdown to Space War̶
By Bhupendra Jasani an̶
ISBN 0 85066 261 3. 104 ̶

For additional information̶
research activities write to:̶

Information Department
SIPRI
Pipers Väg 28
S-171 73 Solna
Sweden